BlackBerry Soul

presents

BlackBerry Soul Celebrations

A Handbook for African-American Bridal and Baby Showers

Kimberly K. Smith

BlackBerry Soul Celebrations:
A Handbook for African-American Bridal and Baby Showers

By Kimberly K. Smith

Published by

BlackBerry Soul
P.O. Box 23821
Washington, DC 20026-3821
Publisher: Kimberly K. Smith
info@blackberrysoul.com
www.blackberrysoul.com

Cover Design: LaVon Jackson, Trinity Consulting Web Design www.lavonjackson.com

Cover art direction: Kimberly K. Smith

Interior Design and Layout: Kimberly K. Smith

Illustrations: *Nighttime Nibbling* and *Shoe Fetish* - iam bennu

Clipart: www.clipart.com, ClipArt with Color™, Images in Black™

What people have said about
BlackBerry Soul Celebrations

"Don't plan your next bridal or baby shower without Blackberry Soul Celebrations. Every mom, sister, aunt, and girlfriend should have a copy on hand to get inspiring ideas for an ethnic shower worth remembering."

Jennifer James
Editor, Mommy Too! Magazine

"This book will be used at many baby showers and bridal showers to come. It was a lot of fun and the themes were right on time. What was most likable about the book was the fact that the images were of black people and the questions focused on themes and people that the black community relate to.

Many times I have been to a baby shower and the host was not able to find many games that kept the interest of the visitors, but with this book you could never run out of the fun.

Kimberly Smith has put a book of questions and answers that we would have runaway from in school and made them fun!!!

***** Stars and congratulations on a job well done!!!"

Heather Elitou
co-Founder, Neshee Publication

"BlackBerry Soul offers a refreshing how and help book for those who want to plan fantastic wedding showers and baby showers. Now, the industry has a collection of exciting, fun and innovative ways to make sure these events are a huge success- with a splash of color. And, this guide offers creative and inexpensive ways to make any gathering a success."

Dion Magee
President, National Black Bridal Association of America

This book is dedicated in loving memory to

Lena and Joe King
and
Mary Lois Smith,

my grandparents whose loving spirits give me strength.

I love and miss you.

This book is a tribute to Black women of all spectrums of the rainbow.

In his 1942 poem "Harlem Sweeties," Langston Hughes rhapsodizes about the rich variety of black beauty visible on a walk through Harlem's famed Sugar Hill.

Have you dug the spill
Of Sugar Hill?
Cast your gims
On this sepia thrill:
Brown sugar lassie,
Caramel treat,
Honey-gold baby
Sweet enough to eat.
Peach-skinned girlie,
Coffee and cream,
Chocolate darling
Out of a dream.
Walnut tinted
Or cocoa brown,
Pomegranate-lipped
Pride of the town.
Rich cream-colored
To plum-tinted black,
Feminine sweetness
In Harlem's no lack.
Glow of the quince
To blush of the rose.
Persimmon bronze
To cinnamon toes.
Blackberry cordial,
Virginia Dare wine --
All those sweet colors
Flavor Harlem of mine!
Walnut or cocoa,
Let me repeat:
Caramel, brown sugar,
A chocolate treat.
Molasses taffy,
Coffee and cream,
Licorice, clove, cinnamon
To a honey-brown dream.
Ginger, wine-gold,
Persimmon, blackberry,
All through the spectrum
Harlem girls vary-
So if you want to know beauty's
Rainbow-sweet thrill,
Stroll down luscious,
Delicious, fine Sugar Hill

Contents

Contents

Acknowledgements

I am forever grateful to be blessed with a loving family who has supported me throughout this process. For six years they have encouraged me as I put my thoughts on paper, put them back on the bookshelf and dusted them off again.

To my husband Reggie who stood by my side, looked over my shoulder and offered lots of suggestions, I love you. To my son, Kyle, "Mommy loves you!" and wishes you could type on the computer for me. Thank you both for being patient when I spent hours capturing my thoughts and ideas on paper.

To my parents Willie and Corine King whose wisdom and strength guides me along, thank you for lovingly nudging me when my energy to complete this book started running out. Mom, you loved my writing ever since I was a little girl; I hope I can continue to make you proud. Thank you both for the emotional, spiritual and financial support you give endlessly to make my dreams come true.

To Marcus, Sandra and Deisha King, my brother and his family, I love you. I can't image life without you guys and who knows, one day we'll move to Florida.

Aunt Ava Forrest, I can't say thank you enough for being my wedding coordinator. Uncle Frank Smith, I can still hear your melodious voice throughout the church. We had a ball that year on St. Croix. Hugs and kisses to the rest of the Smith family, Uncles Victor and O.T. Jr. in Alabama and Aunt Toni in Georgia.

To my cousins, the Dudley Family in Baltimore, Maryland, Sharon, Gaston, Nia and Lee, thank you for always welcoming us to your home.

To Mellonee Simon, my godmother, thank you for showering me with so much love. A special hug and kiss on the cheek for Doris Brodhurst, the wonderful woman who showed me how to use my first curling iron.

Another hug and kiss on the cheek goes to Thelma Moorehead of St. Croix, U.S. Virgin Islands, who makes a rumcake to die for and Veronica Coates for hosting my bridal shower in her beautiful home on St. Croix.

To all of my mother's sorors of Delta Sigma Theta Sorority, Inc. on St. Croix who helped her prepare for my wedding and the marvelous reception that followed, you did a fabulous job!

Thank you to Lori Bryant, Charlette Hudson, and Monica Smith for co-hosting my bridal shower in Maryland.

To my in-laws, Charles and Julia Smith who welcomed me into their family seven years ago, thank you for being the inspiration for some of the games in the book. I'm especially grateful to the numerous McMichael family members in South Carolina, Maryland, and Washington, DC who always welcome me with open arms.

To my other nieces and nephews who keep me smiling, Aunt Kim is grateful to have each one of you in her family.

To the Beard Family over in Germany, be safe and come home soon, we miss you. To Arlene, my girl, I miss your cooking. We've been friends since high school and you've stood by my side through the good and bad.

To Kwame Alexander, author of **Do the Write Thing**, thank you for believing in my project and me. Your expertise and guidance encouraged me to put forth my best.

To Karyn Langhorne Wynn, your editorial expertise was enlightening!

Thank you LaVon Jackson of Trinity Consulting in Dallas, Texas for your creative genius. Your input and insight has made this project shine.

And to all the creative people I've met along the path to publishing success, thank you for your advice.

Introduction

$\mathscr{C}$ongratulations on your upcoming event! Whether you are planning a shower for the new bride or the new mom, *BlackBerry Soul Celebrations: A Handbook for Bridal and Baby Showers* gives African-American women a recipe for planning a memorable affair. The main ingredients that make this handbook essential in your preparation process are two cups of Shower Planning, one cup of Bridal Showers, one cup of Baby Showers, and a pinch of Resources. Each of these combined ingredients can be used to create a special memory for your guest-of-honor. Sprinkled with enlightening wedding facts and quotes from famous African Americans, this book crafts a formula for an entertaining event.

In *BlackBerry Soul Celebrations* you will find a plethora of themes, games and party planning worksheets to prepare you for hosting an impressive occasion. It is filled with games that relate to every day life in the African-American community and themes flavored with the African-American culture that will allow you to provide the bride and groom as well as the mother-to-be with practical things they can use. As many of the showers held today are unisex, where married couples, singles and children are in attendance, the flexibility of this book allows you to cater to a wide audience. Planning a shower can be an intimidating task, but for many, having all the details spelled out clearly as they are in the following pages, makes the responsibilities and difficulties of shower planning melt away.

If your guests would be more comfortable at a quiet sit-down event or would rather laugh and talk loudly there are a multitude of ideas to select from. Use this one-of-a-kind book to select games which will suit the style and taste of your guests in such categories as: Television and Movies, Celebrities, Hip-hop and Old School Music, Sports and the Arts, Global Culture, and Nursery Rhymes. Photocopy the games directly from the book for your affair. If you and your girlfriends are lucky enough to convince your men to give up their weekend sporting event to attend a shower then congratulations are in order. Celebrate those courageous men by playing games from the *Especially for the Brothers* section, which are a tribute to the African-American man. See how well both the men and women at your event remember a few of television's favorite father figures such as Cliff Huxtable, James Evans, Bernie Mac and Michael Kyle.

Enjoy and have fun!

Part 1
SHOWER
PLANNING

Hosting a baby or bridal shower can be a piece of cake. By adding a cup of creativity, a teaspoon of patience, a sprinkle of love, and a dash of energy, you can create a recipe for shower success. The details of planning a shower will blend easily if you are well prepared.

HOSTESS CHECKLIST

Here are some of the ingredients for a well-planned shower:

☑ Guest List

☑ Budget

☑ Theme

☑ Location and Date

☑ Invitations

☑ Menu

☑ Cake

☑ Decorations / Supplies

☑ Party Favors

☑ Games

☑ Thank You Cards / Guest Book

HELPFUL HINT

Each shower is unique so some things may or may not apply to your event.

Guest List

The key ingredient for the shower is the guest list. It is important to know how many people will be invited. If any other showers are planned for the guest-of-honor, try not to duplicate the guest list. You don't want to invite someone who has already been invited to a shower for the same person. Duplicate invitations may make a guest feel obligated to purchase more than one gift for the guest of honor. Keep your Guest List handy, as you will have some decisions to make that will be based on this information.

The Guest List Worksheet in Part 4, Resources will help you track the names, addresses, and other essential information needed for a successful event.

Budget

Determine your budget. A low budget shower can turn out to be a very elegant affair, while the unlimited budget does not guarantee that the party will be a success. The difference is in the planning.   If you are concerned with your budget, then you may look for co-hosts, or ask family members for contributions.

Once you are armed with your financial information, determine how much you will spend in each area. Write a list of the things that you will need, making certain to set aside enough money for the critical items. The Shopping List provided in the Resources Section can help you prioritize the items needed for the event.

The following things may appear on your Shopping List.

- ✓ Location (restaurant, rented club house, etc.)
- ✓ Menu
- ✓ Decorations
- ✓ Party Favors
- ✓ Games and prizes
- ✓ Special Touches
- ✓ Cake
- ✓ Gifts
- ✓ Beverages
- ✓ Cost for rental items (tables, chairs, etc.)
- ✓ Invitations
- ✓ Utensils (forks, knives, etc.)
- ✓ Plates and Napkins

With your list finalized, *divide your funds.*   Look at each item and decide what you would be willing to spend on it.   If you get to the bottom of the list and you have run out of funds, then go back and reconsider some dollar amounts. Typically food and location are the most expensive items.   Look back at the guest list for some guidance. Sometimes size does matter!

If you have a smaller group, you could hold the event at someone's house, and maybe spend a bit more on the menu. Larger groups usually fair well with a simpler menu, and will possibly require renting space for the event. The guest list will also affect some of the other items found on your list, like plates, napkins, and party favors.

Once you have a working budget, you may start the party planning. Don't be afraid to change your budget or task list as you go. It is impossible to predict exactly how the planning will go at this point. And you may find the perfect cake displayed at your local bakery but it may cost a lot more than you want to spend. By finding a great deal on the party favors, that allows you to contribute any extra dollars to your cake fund. Remember that keeping your budget fluid lets you make changes as necessary.

The Budget Planning Worksheet in Part 4 will help you keep track of the items and their associated costs.

Theme

Before deciding on the theme for the shower there are a few things to be considered. First, consider the guest-of-honor. Is she your best friend or a co-worker? In some cases you may want to plan a different shower depending on whom your guest-of- honor will be. **How well you know your guest-of-honor, her tastes, her friends and others involved in the shower will be important considerations in selecting a theme.** Depending on if you are planning a baby or bridal shower there are theme ideas included in the next sections for showers of all sizes, locations and ages.

Next, bear in mind the number of guests that will be in attendance. Will the group be small, large, young, or a mix of people? The games and themes provided in this book can accommodate showers held in small homes or the work environment. By using the games provided in this handbook, you can captivate both the traditional female-only shower and a mixed crowd.

Location and Date

Generally, a shower is held anywhere from 2 to 8 weeks from either a baby's due date, or a wedding date. Saturdays and Sundays are normally the best days of the week that most of your guests will be available. Get in touch with people to be sure that they are available on the days that you are considering. You wouldn't want to plan a Bridal Shower when the Mother-of-the-Bride is on vacation, and be absolutely sure that the guest-of-honor can attend. Contact any guests that may live out of town to inform them of the tentative plan. These people may need extra time to make travel arrangements. Have a couple of possible dates in mind when you research possible locations for your shower. You may have to sacrifice a day or two because the place that you want to rent is not available.

Location is a critical ingredient of a shower. With your guest list, budget, theme, and your date options in hand, choose a place to hold your event that is large enough to accommodate your group, but not too big. Locations that are too large can make a shower seem stiff and formal. Keep in mind any special needs that guests may have, like wheel chair accessibility. Look at the location for anything to tie the natural decor to your party theme.   Locations with decorative elements that support your theme may enhance the shower atmosphere and save you money on décor. For example, if your guest-of-honor is a fitness buff you may try to plan her shower at her favorite gym or health spa. You may also decide to hold the shower at your home or at a restaurant, but again, be sure that there is enough space for the crowd that you will be entertaining. You may also want to consider transportation to your location. Is there public transportation nearby? Is parking convenient? The Location Planning Worksheet in the Resources section can be used to help you plan the location for your event.

Invitations

Make sure that you have the correct addresses and phone numbers for the people on your list. If you are uncertain, start making some phone calls to confirm addresses and phone numbers. Use this list to send out invitations, to track RSVP responses, and then to call those who have not responded.

Choose invitations appropriate for your event. Invitations are usually sent out about 4-6 weeks before the event, and the RSVP date is set to be about a week beforehand. The invitation should give the guest an idea of what to expect. An elegant invitation would represent an elegant affair. A more casual, fun or funky invitation will promise a very different party. There are many options to choose from at your local party supply store, on-line, and in specialty shops, or you could venture to make your own. The invitation should include the purpose of the event, location, time, date, an RSVP date, and your phone number. Consider including a map or directions to the shower site. On-line sites such as www.evite.com have free electronic invitations that you can send to your guests. This particular site not only offers several different styles of shower invitations but will also allow users to send a map to the event location as well as track RSVPs. Another on-line source to create a map to your event is www.mapquest.com. Be sure to tell guests if the shower is a surprise. The Guest List Worksheet described in the previous section will help you track the invitations sent.

Menu

The menu can be a bit tricky. Will the event be catered or will you make your own food? Should you serve a meal or finger foods? Will it be buffet or sit-down? What food items will your guests most likely to enjoy? The possibilities are endless. **Your menu will largely depend on the location selected, number of guests, and budget.** If a restaurant is selected as the shower location, then it could be as simple as going through the menu with the restaurant manager.   If not, you've got some

> ### DID YOU KNOW?
>
> At the wedding reception of Mary J. Blige and Kendu Isaacs on December 7, 2003, guests were served oxtail, barbecue chicken, crab, red rice and salad.
>
> www.usatoday.com

work to do. Look again at the size of your group and your budget. If you are going to cater the meal, contact caterers as soon as possible. Most caterers have a menu that they can fax or mail to you. If you choose to prepare food yourself, be sure that you will have the needed equipment at the party location (i.e. stove, refrigerator, etc). Think of any menu items that may support your theme.

Cake

Another essential ingredient to the shower is the decision to either make or buy a cake. If baking is not your strong point, consider purchasing a cake from your local grocery store or bakery. These professionals offer cakes in a wide selection of sizes, colors and flavors. Your local grocery store or bakery will also be able to recommend the size of the cake suitable for the total number of guests expected. If there is a family member or close friend of the guest-of-honor who is a reputable baker, consider asking him or her to bake the cake. Keep in mind the size of the cake so that there will be enough for your guests as well as extra slices for the guest-of-honor to take home. In my experience guests may take as many as two extra slices to loved ones at home.

Decorations/Supplies

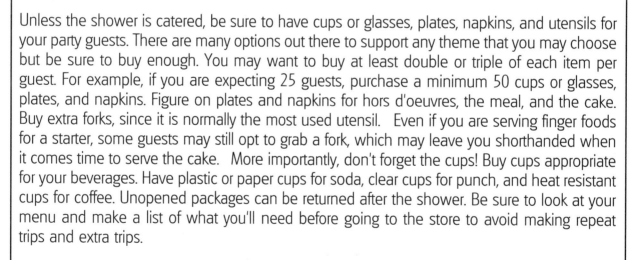

Decorations should coordinate with the theme of the party. Determine what decorations will be appropriate for the location of the shower. Clubhouses may have restrictions on pin-up decorations, while some restaurants may only allow balloons. Visit your local party supply store or go on-line for items such as balloons, streamers, centerpieces, and anything else that contributes to your party's theme. Try not to go overboard. In some cases, less is more.

Unless the shower is catered, be sure to have cups or glasses, plates, napkins, and utensils for your party guests. There are many options out there to support any theme that you may choose but be sure to buy enough. You may want to buy at least double or triple of each item per guest. For example, if you are expecting 25 guests, purchase a minimum 50 cups or glasses, plates, and napkins. Figure on plates and napkins for hors d'oeuvres, the meal, and the cake. Buy extra forks, since it is normally the most used utensil. Even if you are serving finger foods for a starter, some guests may still opt to grab a fork, which may leave you shorthanded when it comes time to serve the cake. More importantly, don't forget the cups! Buy cups appropriate for your beverages. Have plastic or paper cups for soda, clear cups for punch, and heat resistant cups for coffee. Unopened packages can be returned after the shower. Be sure to look at your menu and make a list of what you'll need before going to the store to avoid making repeat trips and extra trips.

Party Favors

Most Baby and Bridal Showers offer guests some sort of party favor. ***Favors can be as little or as large as you'd like, simple or extravagant.*** It's a way of saying "thank you for attending".

In selecting favors there are two options. You can either make favors if you have the time, creativity and resources, or purchase pre-made favors. In either of your selections, try to have personalized items that tie into the theme of the party, or add a special note, or even just a name and date written on the bottom of the item.

Games

Baby and Bridal Showers usually bring together a mix of friends, neighbors, co-workers and family members, and the guest-of-honor is often so overwhelmed by the event that formal introductions are missed. ***Games offer guests the opportunity to get to know each other as well as a chance to celebrate the occasion.*** The games offered in Parts 2 and 3 of this book are not only engaging, but will reflect your guests' lifestyles, traditions and values. Games are offered in a wide range of topics and themes relevant to their interests. As an added treat, consider purchasing prizes for your game winners. Great finds can be found at your local dollar store, or the clearance racks at the malls. Wrap treasures in colorful wrapping paper or decorated gift bags and you are ready to reward your winners. Have one or two extra gifts available in case a game ends in a tie.

Thank You Cards / Guest Book

Purchase Thank You cards that coordinate with the event's theme. These should be sent to the people who have helped you to host the event. In addition, you may also consider purchasing cards for the guest-of-honor so that she will be able to thank the guests for attending. Pass on the guest list to the guest-of-honor to be sure that she has the correct phone numbers and addresses for her Thank You cards. A guest book is a good way to record each shower attendee and the gift given by that attendee. It is also records the best address for the guest-of-honor to send Thank You cards. If you don't have a guest book, the Guest List Worksheet included in the Resources section can be used for this purpose.

NOTES

Part 2
BRIDAL SHOWERS

The themes and games included in this section are appropriate for different types of showers, Whether you are planning an energetic bash or a quiet sit-down event there is something suited for your taste.

Themes in this portion of the book range from peaceful and tranquil to wild and zany. You will be able to select from a <u>Scents and Fragrances Shower</u> where guests bring scented candles and tropical fragrances to an <u>Exotic Shower</u> where guests are encouraged to bring flavored lingerie.

Games in this section will test your guests' knowledge of Kwanzaa traditions, R&B love songs, and some of Hollywood's hottest Black celebrity couples.

Chapter 1
BRIDAL SHOWER THEMES

Around the Clock

Before the shower, assign each guest a specific hour of the day, and choose a gift that could be used at that particular time. For example, an alarm clock to be used at six a.m., a coffee maker used at seven a.m., or a silk bathrobe, which might be used at eleven p.m. Even though there are no specific games that match this theme, you might consider playing any of the games included in the next section.

Bon Voyage

Select items the bride will need on her honeymoon. If the newlyweds are planning to visit a Caribbean destination they may need disposable cameras to take lots of pictures or a new set of luggage. Beach towels and cover-ups are sure to make a splash. If the couple will be in a colder climate, perhaps they would appreciate ski parkas, gloves, or scarves. Although there are no particular games that correspond with this theme, your guests will enjoy playing any of the ones included in the next section.

Colors

For this type of shower, guests are assigned a color. Gifts for the bride-to-be must be of the specified color. Another variation of a color-themed shower is to provide the couple with items in their favorite colors. Any of the games included in the next section could be played if this theme is selected.

Decorative Art

African statues and figurines are sure to complement any house or apartment. If you want to shop on-line visit Ethnic Home Décor at http://ethnichomedecor.com/. There are also a variety of prints available on-line from African-American artists. You can purchase a print from the guest-of-honor's favorite artist at the following on-line sites: www.brownhorizonsart.com, www.heritagesart.com, and www.africanartworld.com. There are also many other sites that offer works from various artists in different styles. Even though Capturing Creativity may be the only games associated with this particular theme, all of the games included in the next section could be played at this style of shower.

Erotic

An erotic shower makes a great combination bridal shower and bachelorette party, since the bride receives gifts that will certainly add some excitement to the couple's honeymoon. Massage oils, glow-in-the-dark underclothing, handcuffs, or sexy lingerie are a few items worth considering. Games in the section that add to this theme include Genuine Gentlemen, Gentlemen's Delight, Hip Hop Hotties, and Groom's Game Part II.

Favorite Room in the House

At this shower, the bride will select the room(s) in the house she would like her guests to help her decorate. If she needs help decorating the bathroom, coordinated shower curtains, rugs, towels, and hampers make great gifts. For the kitchen, appliances such as toasters, coffee makers, blenders, or silverware are good choices. Comforters, sheets, pillows, and blankets for the bedroom can also make great gifts. Any of the games included in the next section could be played if this theme is selected.

Fitness

For the couple that wants to stay physically fit, a shower with a fitness theme will surely be applauded. Gift memberships to health clubs, roller blades, or mountain bikes can help keep the newlyweds in shape. If the bride prefers videos, fitness expert Donna Richardson is among many of the top fitness trainers that offer a selection of workout tapes. One particular game in the section that enhances this theme is Awesome Athletes.

Gourmet Foods

For the couple that enjoys a culinary treat, gourmet wines, coffees, popcorn, and cheeses are sure to be appreciated by the newlyweds. There are a variety of fine wines and gourmet cheeses that will add a zestful flavor to any meal. On-line resources, which will help in your selection of gourmet items, include www.williams-sonoma.com, www.gevalia.com, and www.igourmet.com. In the next section, games such as Down Homes Dishes and Caribbean Cuisine will boost your theme.

DID YOU KNOW?

Kola nuts play an important role in African weddings. The nut, which is used for medicinal purposes in Africa, represents the couple's and their families' willingness to always help heal each other.

www.mdblackweddings.com

Lingerie

For this type of shower, select lingerie that the bride will enjoy wearing on her honeymoon. Request that guests purchase sexy items from her favorite lingerie store, which will complement the newlywed's figure. These items are certain to add excitement to the honeymoon. Themes that coincide with this type of shower include Genuine Gentlemen, Gentlemen's Delight, Hip Hop Hotties, and Groom's Game Part II.

Musical

Have guests purchase compact discs or cassettes of the couple's favorite musical groups or different genres of music. Gifts may include a compact disc player, home stereo, or concert tickets for the newlyweds. Musical themed games such as <u>Smooth Sounds</u>, <u>Divine Divas</u>, <u>Charming Crooners</u>, and <u>Macho Musicians</u> will highlight this theme.

New Home
Perhaps the bride and groom are considering home ownership. Many banks around the country are now willing to set up a home mortgage fund where guests can donate money towards the couple's down payment. Although there are no specific games that correspond with this theme, you might consider playing any of the games included in the next section.

Pampered Pair
Gift certificates for day spa treatments such as facials, massages, pedicures, or manicures are just the things to help the couple feel relaxed and pampered before their wedding day. Games created with couples in mind include <u>Matrimonial Matches Part I and Part II</u> and <u>Powerful Partnerships</u>.

Personalized Items
Items such as door knockers, towels, or robes personalized with the couple's name or initials are sure to be appreciated. Another useful gift may be decorative mailing labels with the couple's name and address. Even if there are no specific games that fit this theme, your guests will enjoy playing any of the games included in the next section.

Rites of Passage
Candles, incense, and hot tea can be used to provide a relaxing atmosphere where the bride and shower guests can reminisce about how they met, the reasons they were attracted to each other, and the crazy things that have happened along the way. Or, if you wish to follow African culture, consider a "rite of passage" ceremony where the female elders tell the bride what to expect and help orient her about the realities of married life. Games in the section that add to this theme include <u>Kwanzaa Dilemma</u>, <u>Cultural Trivia</u>, and <u>Traditional Custom</u>.

Scents and Fragrances
Select oils, colognes, or powders in the bride's favorite scents. If the bride enjoys natural scents, several can be used to achieve various objectives.
To restore energy and as a pick-me-up, the bride might try a few whiffs of lemon, grapefruit, rosemary, or peppermint. She can use these scents to feel rejuvenated after planning her wedding. To relieve frustration, the calming scents of lavender, chamomile and neroli aid in relaxing the mind and body. To set a romantic mood, the new bride might use scents of gardenia, mandarin orange, jasmin, and ylangylng. Other pleasing aromas can be found in geranium, thyme, basil, and clary sage. Although there are no specific games related to this

DID YOU KNOW?

Among the G'wi of Botswana, the bride-to-be fasts in silence for four days outside the village and then has her head shaved and is bathed by the female elders.

www.weddingchannel.com

theme, select a game from the next section that will complement the taste and interest of your guests.

Sorority/Fraternity

Many couples are members of African-American Greek letter organizations, some of which originated at various historically black universities. The sisters of Delta Sigma Theta, Inc. and the brothers of Kappa Alpha Psi Fraternity, Inc. would both enjoy crimson and cream-colored paraphernalia. An elephant would be an ideal gift for the Delta woman. The men of Omega Psi Phi Fraternity, Inc. may appreciate paraphernalia in purple and gold. The women of Alpha Kappa Alpha Sorority, Inc. would appreciate salmon pink and apple green items, and the sisters of Zeta Phi Beta, Inc. would enjoy royal blue and white-colored paraphernalia. The ladies of Sigma Gamma Rho Sorority, Inc. enjoy royal blue and gold-colored items while the men of Phi Beta Sigma Fraternity, Inc. would appreciate blue and white-colored paraphernalia. On-line resources to order paraphernalia include www.simplygreek.com and www.greek4life.com. Although there are no specific Greek-related games that match this theme, you might consider playing Sensational Sisterhood and Powerful Partnerships.

Spiritual

In keeping with healing the mind, body and soul, the newlyweds may wish to have a spiritual shower. Aromatherapy has long been recognized as an ancient healing art. By inhaling specific fragrances the body's muscles can be relaxed. One such fragrance, lavender, can be used to relieve stress and headaches. Other gifts to complement a spiritual shower could include herbal teas, fragrant candles, and potpourri. Self-help and spiritual awareness books by authors such as Iyanla Vanzant, Bishop T.D. Jakes, and Prophetess Juanita Bynum cover such topics as building relationships and incorporating spiritual principles into your life. Although there are no games designed specifically for this type of shower, your guests will be amused after playing any of the games included.

> ### DID YOU KNOW?
>
> Many cultures also perform purification rituals to cleanse the body and soul of any impurities that either partner might bring to the relationship. For Zulu women, it's customary for the bride and her female companions to bathe together on her wedding morning.
>
> www.weddingchannel.com

Sports

Shower the couple with items relating to their favorite sports team. Season tickets, jackets, coffee mugs, or t-shirts with their team logo are sure to keep their competitive spirit high. One particular game in the section that adds to this theme is Awesome Athletes.

Through the Year

Prior to the shower, assign each guest a month and instruct him or her to bring a gift that suits a particular celebration in that month. Consider giving some of the writings of Dr. Martin Luther King Jr., whose birthday is an official holiday in the month of January. Other gifts may include a clock for the ringing in of a New Year or a heart-shaped crystal box in commemoration of Valentine's Day in February. A book about Kwanzaa, which is celebrated in December, may be the gift that begins a family tradition for the newlyweds. Kwanzaa Dilemma or Anniversary Gifts are games suited for this theme.

What's Cookin'?

If the newlyweds need a little assistance in the kitchen with meal planning or preparation, cookbooks or recipe ideas may be just the help they need. Write down your favorite recipes or provide the couple with cookbooks from different parts of the world. Cookbooks, which focus on Caribbean, Creole, or soul foods, can be found in your local bookstore. Special seasonings such as saffron and curry used frequently in the Caribbean are sure to  accentuate the flavor of any dish. Cooking lessons or a week's chef service are gifts that will also be enjoyed by the newlyweds. In the next section, games such as Down Home Dishes and Caribbean Cuisine will boost your theme.

DID YOU KNOW?

Tasting the elements: Adapted from a Yoruba tradition, the bride and groom taste flavors that represent the different emotions within a relationship: sour (lemon), bitter (vinegar), hot (cayenne), and sweet (honey), for example. This symbolizes the couple's ability to get through the hard times in life to enjoy the sweetness of marriage.

www.essence.com

Chapter 2
BRIDAL SHOWER GAMES

HELPFUL HINT

Prior to the shower select the games you will use for your event. To ensure you have enough copies for each of your guests, make at least 5 extra copies per game. For example, if you expect 20 people to attend, make at least 25 copies per game.

GENTLEMEN'S DELIGHT

CELEBRITIES

Name these gorgeous divas whose names will no longer be on the lips of the groom-to-be.

1. In the 2003 comedy <u>Deliver Us From Eva</u>, she played the starring role as Eva.

   _____

2. This five-time Grammy award winner also starred in the 2003 comedy, <u>The Fighting Temptations</u>.

   _____

3. This multi-talented superstar has appeared in <u>Poetic Justice</u> and <u>The Nutty Professor II</u>.

   _____

4. In 2001, her first album <u>Songs in A Minor</u> garnered two NAACP Image Awards.

   _____

5. This promising actress and musician's career was tragically cut short by her death in a plane crash.

   _____

6. She was the first to bring a feminist consciousness to rap's political agenda with her 1989 debut, <u>All Hail the Queen</u>.

   _____

7. This Canadian artist was nominated for a Grammy Award for <u>You've Put A Move On My Heart</u>.

   _____

8. Her self-titled debut album included the following songs: <u>What's Luv?</u>, <u>Always on Time</u>, and <u>Foolish</u>.

   _____

9. She starred opposite Mario Van Peebles in <u>Posse</u> and the hit CBS show <u>Family Law</u>.

   _____

10. She is the ex-wife of Duane Martin in the 2003 television show <u>All of Us</u>.

    _____

GENTLEMEN'S
DELIGHT

A
N
S
W
E
R
S

1. Gabrielle Union

2. Beyonce Knowles

3. Janet Jackson

4. Alicia Keys

5. Aaliyah

6. Queen Latifah also known as Dana Owens

7. Tamia

8. Ashanti

9. Sally Richardson

10. LisaRaye McCoy

GENUINE
GENTLEMEN

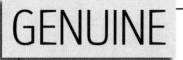

CELEBRITIES

List these eye-catching gentlemen that the bride-to-be will no longer be able to stare at?

1. He is an Academy Award winner whose movie credits include <u>Crimson Tide</u> and <u>Glory.</u>

    _____

2. As attorney Jonathan Rollins on <u>L.A. Law</u>, he won a NAACP Image Award.

    _____

3. His hit record albums include <u>Keep It Comin'</u> and <u>Make It Last Forever.</u>

    _____

4. His first smash hit <u>One Last Cry</u> can be found on his 1992 debut album.

    _____

5. One of his most well known roles was Malcolm on <u>The Young and the Restless.</u>

    _____

6. His famous lines in the 1991 hit movie, <u>New Jack City</u>: *"Am I my brother's keeper?"*

    _____

7. This former <u>New York Undercover</u> star was also a Jamaican bobsledder in the movie <u>Cool Runnings</u>.

    _____

8. This former New Edition member also joined the R&B Music group, LSG.

    _____

9. He's widely known for portraying Neil Winters on the soap opera, <u>The Young and Restless</u>.

    _____

10. This Grammy Award winning rapper starred in his own television show <u>In The House</u>.

    _____

GENUINE
GENTLEMEN

ANSWERS

1. Denzel Washington
2. Blair Underwood
3. Keith Sweat
4. Brian McKnight
5. Shemar Moore
6. Wesley Snipes
7. Malik Yoba
8. Johnny Gill
9. Kristoff St. John
10. James Todd Smith a.k.a. LL Cool J

HIP-HOP
HOTTIES

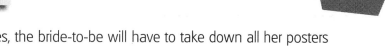

CELEBRITIES

As the wedding day approaches, the bride-to-be will have to take down all her posters of these bad boys of hip-hop and rap. *Can you help her to identify these hotties of hip-hop?*

1. Although he may profess to be a <u>Gigolo</u>, he had the starring role in <u>Drumline</u>.

    _____

2. The stars of <u>You Got Served </u>also made such hits as <u>Bump, Bump, Bump</u> and <u>Gots Ta Be</u>.

    _____

3. This heartthrob's hits include <u>You Make Me Wanna</u>, <u>Yeah</u>, and <u>My Way</u>.

    _____

4. This star from the Dirty South had a starring role in <u>2 Fast 2 Furious</u>.

    _____

5. This God's Son's song <u>I Can</u> has been sung by kids around the country.

    _____

6. This rapper's thuggish style created harmonies in duets with Jennifer Lopez and Ashanti.

    _____

7. This rapper's hit tracks include <u>In Da Club</u> and <u>P.I.M.P.</u>

    _____

8. He may be <u>Still Ghetto</u>, but this singer advises us to <u>Put That Woman First</u>.

    _____

9. This <u>Ruff Ryder</u> has appeared in movies alongside Aaliyah and Gabrielle Union.

    _____

10. This famous rapper starred in <u>Like Mike</u> and <u>Johnson Family Vacation</u>.

    _____

HIP-HOP HOTTIES

ANSWERS

1. Nick Cannon

2. B2K – group members J-Boog (Jarell Damonte Houston), Raz-B (De'mario Monte Thornton), Lil' Fizz (Druex Pierre Fredericks), and Omarion (Omari Ishmael Grandberry)

3. Usher Raymond IV

4. Ludacris also known as Christopher Bridges

5. Nas also known as Nasir Jones

6. Ja Rule also known as Jeffrey Atkins

7. 50 Cents also known as Curtis Jackson

8. Jaheim Hoagland

9. DMX also known as Earl Simmons

10. Bow Wow also known as Shad Gregory Moss

HOT
HUNKS

CELEBRITIES

Identify these eye-catching gentlemen that the bride-to-be will now have to worship secretly.

1. _____

He gained national attention for his debut role as Ricky Baker in <u>Boyz 'N The Hood</u>. He also starred in the movies <u>The Best Man</u> and <u>The Brothers</u>.

2. _____

As William Shakespeare, he married Angela Bassett in the movie <u>How Stella Got Her Groove.</u>

3. _____

In the movie, <u>Love Jones</u>, this actor played the leading role alongside Nia Long.

4. _____

His big screen credits include <u>The Wood</u>, <u>Higher Learning</u>, and <u>The Mod Squad</u>.

5. _____

His television debut role was as Detective Baldwin Jones on the television drama <u>NYPD Blue</u>.

6. _____

He stood out in the ensemble cast of <u>The Best Man</u> as Quentin, the lovable, but totally jaded musician.

7. _____

He has become one of TV's hottest sex symbols with his starring role as Warrick Brown on the new TV drama series <u>C.S.I.</u>

8. _____

This black-belt martial artist also portrayed boxing champ Mike Tyson in the HBO movie <u>Tyson</u>.

9. _____

He came into the spotlight in the 1992 film <u>Juice</u>. Six years later he portrayed golf legend Tiger Woods in the movie <u>The Tiger Woods Story</u>.

10. _____

This actor formerly appeared as Damon, on Showtime's hit series <u>Soul Food.</u>

HOT
HUNKS

ANSWERS

1. Morris Chestnut
2. Taye Diggs
3. Larenz Tate
4. Omar Epps
5. Henry Simmonds
6. Terrence Howard
7. Gary Dourdan
8. Michael Jai White
9. Khalil Kain
10. Boris Kodjoe

CELEBRITIES

LUSCIOUS
LADIES

As the wedding day approaches the groom-to-be will no longer be able to sit and stare at these foxy ladies. *Can you help him to identify these luscious ladies?*

1. This Oscar winner has also starred in the movies <u>Catwoman</u> and <u>Losing Isaiah</u>.

    _____

2. She played the role of Betty Shabazz both in <u>Malcolm X</u> and in the movie <u>Panther</u>.

    _____

3. This former Miss America has also appeared in the hit action movie <u>Eraser</u>.

    _____

4. She has appeared in the movie <u>Set It Off</u> as well as <u>Kill Bill,</u> Volumes I and II.

    _____

5. The original <u>Foxy Brown</u> actress who also starred in television show <u>The L Word</u>.

    _____

6. <u>Harlem Nights</u> was her movie debut but she can be seen in <u>Waiting to Exhale</u>.

    _____

7. This star of <u>The Nutty Professor</u> can also be seen in <u>The Matrix Reloaded</u>.

    _____

8. This <u>Preacher's Wife</u> actress also won a Grammy Award for her song <u>I Will Always Love You</u>.

    _____

9. She is the host and executive producer of the television show <u>America's Next Top Model</u>.

    _____

10. She sold over ten million copies of her self-titled debut album yet declared bankruptcy.

    _____

LUSCIOUS
LADIES

ANSWERS

1. Halle Berry
2. Angela Bassett
3. Vanessa L. Williams
4. Vivica A. Fox
5. Pam Grier
6. Lela Rochon
7. Jada Pinkett Smith
8. Whitney Houston
9. Tyra Banks
10. Toni Braxton

POWERFUL PARTNERSHIPS

CELEBRITIES

These famous African American couples have had a significant impact on history; see if you can identify them by last name.

1. Ronald and Alma_____
   (Hint: The first African-American Secretary of Commerce, he was killed in a plane crash in 1997. He and his wife had two children, Tracy and Michael.)

2. William and Camille_____
   (Hint: He and his wife have donated several million dollars to Spelman College in Atlanta, Georgia. They have three daughters and a son who was tragically killed in 1997.)

3. Colin and Alma_____
   (Hint: He is a former Chairman of the Joint Chiefs of Staff and Secretary of State. He and his wife have three children, Michael, Linda, and Annemarie.)

4. Reverend Jesse and Alma_____
   (Hint: This civil rights leader ran for president in 1984 and is President of the National Rainbow Coalition.)

5. Nelson and Winnie_____
   (Hint: He won the Nobel Peace Prize in 1993. She is recognized for her dedication to educating the people of Mozambique, and for her leadership in organizations devoted to the children of her war-torn country.)

6. Reverend Dr. Martin Luther and Coretta Scott_____
   (Hint: His birthday is recognized as a national holiday in January. After her husband was assassinated, she continued his work, becoming a great Civil Rights activist. Their children are Bernice, Yolanda, Dexter, and Martin III.)

7. Malcolm and Betty_____
   (Hint: This former minister of the Nation of Islam was assassinated in 1965 at the Audubon Ballroom in Harlem, New York. She died after being severely burned in a fire in her New York apartment in 1997. They had six daughters.)

8. Ossie _____ and Ruby _____
   (Hint: She is an award-winning stage, film and television actress whose Broadway and Off-Broadway performances include A Raisin in the Sun (1959). Originally a stage actor and writer, he later wrote the screenplay for and directed the film Cotton Comes to Harlem (1970), and he has appeared in a number of Spike Lee movies.)

9. Medgar and Myrlie_____
   (Hint: He was the first Field Secretary for the National Association for the Advancement of Colored People (NAACP) and was assassinated in his driveway in 1963. She served as National Chairwoman of the NAACP.)

10. John and Eunice_____
    (Hint: He is the CEO and chairman of the largest black-owned publishing company, publishers of EBONY and JET magazines.)

POWERFUL PARTNERSHIPS

A
N
S
W
E
R
S

1.   Ronald and Alma Brown

2.   William and Camille Cosby

3.   Colin and Alma Powell

4.   Jesse and Alma Jackson

5.   Nelson and (Winnie) Graça Machel Mandela

6.   Martin Luther and Coretta Scott King

7.   (Malcolm) El Hajj Malik el-Shabazz and Betty Shabazz

8.   Ossie Davis and Ruby Dee

9.   Medgar and Myrlie Evers

10.   John and Eunice Johnson

SENSATIONAL
SISTERHOOD

These influential women have left quite a mark on history, paving the way for others to follow in their footsteps. In celebration of sisterhood, **match each woman to her incredible accomplishment.**

1. _____ Dr. Mae Jemison

    a.   Also known as "Moses" she led at least 300 slaves to freedom using the Underground Railroad.

2. _____ Harriett Tubman

    b.   First prominent African American woman to become directly associated with the woman's suffrage movement.

3. _____ Rosa Parks

    c.   This educator founded a school for girls in Daytona Beach, Florida, which became one of the Historically Black Colleges and Universities.

4. _____ Oprah Winfrey

    d.   First black woman millionaire who made her fortune in the beauty and cosmetics industry.

5. _____ Madame C.J. Walker

    e.   First black woman to own her own television studio.

6. _____ Sojourner Truth

    f.   In 2005 she became the first African American women appointed as Secretary of State.

7. _____ Barbara Jordan

    g.   Because of her refusal to give up her seat on the bus, she is considered to be the Mother of the Civil Rights Movement

8. _____ Dr. Condoleeza Rice

    g.   The first black woman elected to the House of Representatives. She gave the keynote address at the 1976 Democratic convention.

9. _____ Mary McCloud Bethune

    i.   The world's first African American female astronaut. She made her first shuttle space flight in the Endeavor in September 1992.

10. _____ Cicely Tyson

    j.   As one of the most respected and honored actors in American theater, film and television, this lady is a seven-time Emmy nominee.

SENSATIONAL
SISTERHOOD

A
N
S
W
E
R
S

1.   i.   Dr. Mae Jemison
2.   a.   Hariett Tubman
3.   g.   Rosa Parks
4.   e.   Oprah Winfrey
5.   d.   Madame C.J. Walker
6.   b.   Sojourner Truth
7.   h.   Barbara Jordan
8.   f.   Dr. Condoleeza Rice
9.   c.   Mary McCloud Bethune
10.   j.   Cicely Tyson

CARIBBEAN CUISINE

"The best way to a man's heart is through his stomach", also rings true in the Caribbean.

How many tasty Caribbean fruits, drinks and spicy dishes can you unscramble?

1. TOATOP GFINFTSU _____

2. RGENIG REBE _____

3. CRURY NICKHEC _____

4. KOAOLLAL _____

5. IUABM _____

6. IGUNF _____

7. ESUSO _____

8. DTANMARI _____

9. YHNOJN KEAC _____

10. TSAL IHSF IUNDG _____

11. OHNCC RRETIFST _____

12. REIFD PNLIAIANT _____

13. SDEEANSO ECIR _____

14. MUR KECA _____

15. RLROSE _____

16. SOPROUS _____

17. GUABAVRYRE URM _____

18. ANIVEN KECA _____

19. KERJ IKCEHNC _____

20. BAANNA RRETIFST _____

CARIBBEAN CUISINE

A
N
S
W
E
R
S

1. POTATO STUFFING
2. GINGER BEER
3. CURRY CHICKEN
4. KALLALOO
5. MUABI
6. FUNGI
7. SOUSE
8. TAMARIND
9. JOHNNY CAKE
10. SALT FISH GUNDI
11. CONCH FRITTERS
12. FRIED PLAINTAIN
13. SEASONED RICE
14. RUM CAKE
15. SORREL
16. SOURSOP
17. GUAVABERRY RUM
18. VIENNA CAKE
19. JERK CHICKEN
20. BANANA FRITTERS

CULTURAL
TRIVIA

GLOBAL
CULTURE

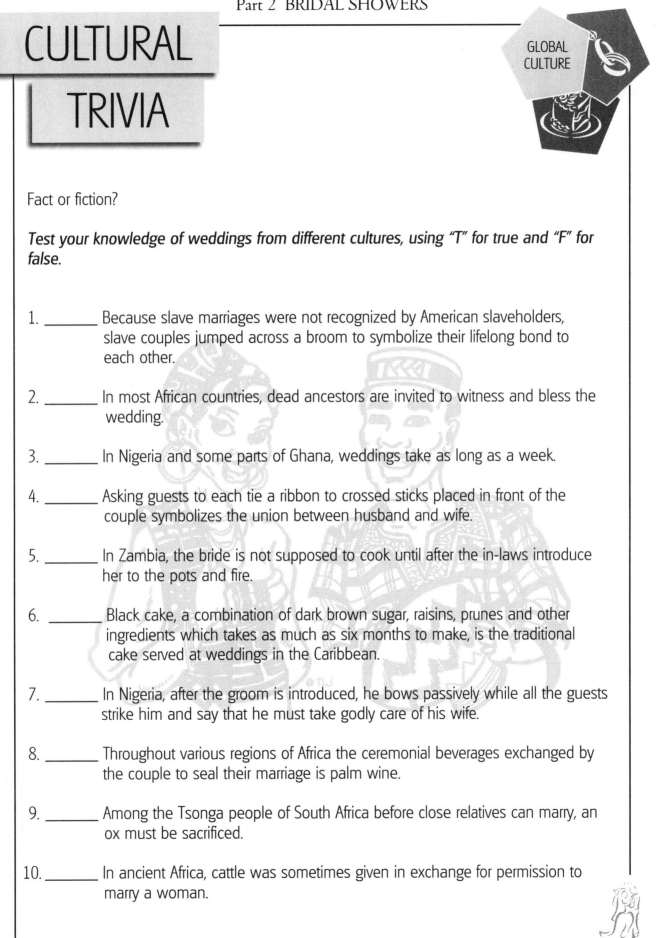

Fact or fiction?

Test your knowledge of weddings from different cultures, using "T" for true and "F" for false.

1. _____ Because slave marriages were not recognized by American slaveholders, slave couples jumped across a broom to symbolize their lifelong bond to each other.

2. _____ In most African countries, dead ancestors are invited to witness and bless the wedding.

3. _____ In Nigeria and some parts of Ghana, weddings take as long as a week.

4. _____ Asking guests to each tie a ribbon to crossed sticks placed in front of the couple symbolizes the union between husband and wife.

5. _____ In Zambia, the bride is not supposed to cook until after the in-laws introduce her to the pots and fire.

6. _____ Black cake, a combination of dark brown sugar, raisins, prunes and other ingredients which takes as much as six months to make, is the traditional cake served at weddings in the Caribbean.

7. _____ In Nigeria, after the groom is introduced, he bows passively while all the guests strike him and say that he must take godly care of his wife.

8. _____ Throughout various regions of Africa the ceremonial beverages exchanged by the couple to seal their marriage is palm wine.

9. _____ Among the Tsonga people of South Africa before close relatives can marry, an ox must be sacrificed.

10. _____ In ancient Africa, cattle was sometimes given in exchange for permission to marry a woman.

CULTURAL TRIVIA

A
N
S
W
E
R
S

1. True
2. True
3. True
4. True
5. True
6. True
7. True
8. True
9. True
10. True

DOWN HOME DISHES

According to the 1996 hit movie *Soul Food*, "soul food is about cooking from the heart."
How many of these tasty soul food dishes can you help the bride-to-be unscramble?

1. HSUAQS _____

2. DIECAND SAMY _____

3. DREIF NKECCIH _____

4. LTEAMFOA _____

5. IACRONMA NAD ESECHE _____

6. CHNTERIGSLTI _____

7. DAMHSE STOEPATO _____

8. CARLOLD ENERGS _____

9. TINSRG BNSEA _____

10. OTAPTO ALSDA _____

11. MPLDUINSG _____

12. OSRAT FEBE _____

13. NRCBODEAR _____

14. CSOLEWAL _____

15. BKCLA DEEY SAEP _____

16. TSWEE OTAPTO EPI _____

17. ANBANA IPNGDUD _____

18. PACEH LROBEBC _____

19. KDABE MAH _____

20. MAIL BNSEA _____

DOWN HOME
DISHES

A
N
S
W
E
R
S

1. SQUASH
2. CANDIED YAMS
3. FRIED CHICKEN
4. MEATLOAF
5. MACARONI AND CHEESE
6. CHITTERLINGS
7. MASHED POTATOES
8. COLLARD GREENS
9. STRING BEANS
10. POTATO SALAD
11. DUMPLINGS
12. ROAST BEEF
13. CORNBREAD
14. COLESLAW
15. BLACK EYED PEAS
16. SWEET POTATO PIE
17. BANANA PUDDING
18. PEACH COBBLER
19. BAKED HAM
20. LIMA BEANS

KWANZAA
DILEMMA

GLOBAL CULTURE

African American households across the world bless December 26 through January 1 with the seven-day observance of Kwanzaa. The newlyweds may want to consider this a family tradition in which one of its members lights a candle for the day's daily principle and a discussion of the family's adaptation of that day's value commences.

Match the correct principle with its meaning.

1. _____ Umoja

a. Unity. To strive and maintain unity in the family, community, nation, and race.

2. _____ Kujichagulia

b. Cooperative Economics. To build and maintain our own stores, shops, and other businesses and to profit from them together.

3. _____ Ujima

c. Faith. To believe with all our heart in our people, our parents, our teachers, our leaders, and the righteousness and victory of our struggle.

4. _____ Ujamma

d. Self-determination. To define ourselves, name ourselves, create ourselves, and speak of ourselves instead of being defined, named, created for, and spoken for by others.

5. _____ Nia

e. Collective Work and Responsibility. To build and maintain our community together and to make our sisters' and brothers' problems our problems and to solve them together.

6. _____ Kuumba

f. Purpose. To make our collective vocation the building and developing of our community to restore our people and their traditional greatness.

7. _____ Imani

g. Creativity. To do always as much as we can, in whatever way we can, to leave our community more beautiful and beneficial than we inherited it.

KWANZAA

DILEMMA

A
N
S
W
E
R
S

1. a. Unity

2. d. Self-determination

3. e. Collective work and responsibility

4. b. Cooperative economics

5. f. Purpose

6. g. Creativity

7. c. Faith

CHARMING
CROONERS

HIP-HOP AND OLD SCHOOL MUSIC

These gentlemen have stirred the hearts of women across the country. Their smooth sounds have brought couples together for more than twenty years.

Match the famous soloist or group to their well-known "love" song.

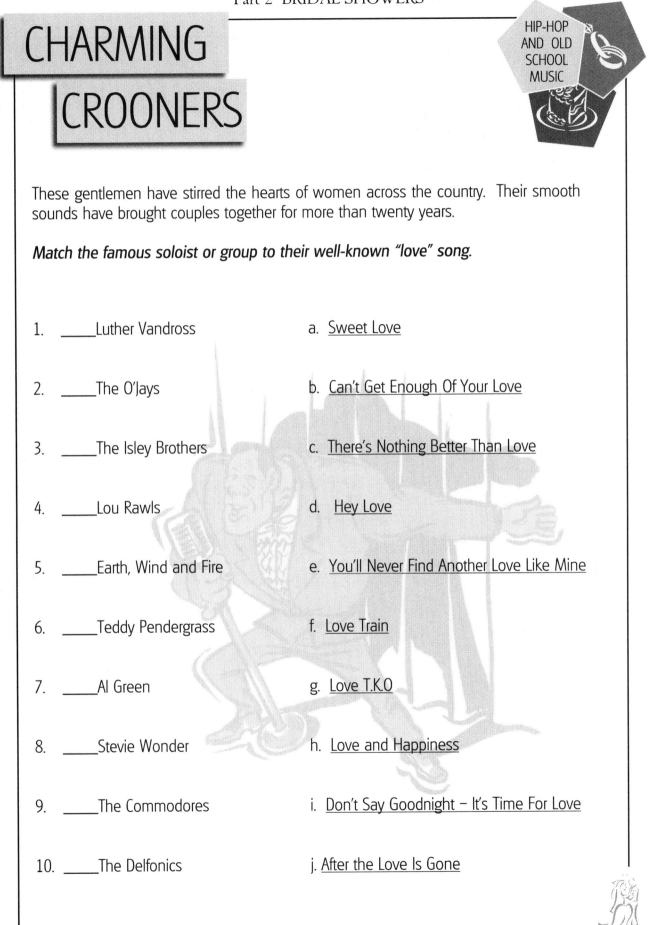

1. _____Luther Vandross   a. <u>Sweet Love</u>

2. _____The O'Jays   b. <u>Can't Get Enough Of Your Love</u>

3. _____The Isley Brothers   c. <u>There's Nothing Better Than Love</u>

4. _____Lou Rawls   d. <u>Hey Love</u>

5. _____Earth, Wind and Fire   e. <u>You'll Never Find Another Love Like Mine</u>

6. _____Teddy Pendergrass   f. <u>Love Train</u>

7. _____Al Green   g. <u>Love T.K.O</u>

8. _____Stevie Wonder   h. <u>Love and Happiness</u>

9. _____The Commodores   i. <u>Don't Say Goodnight – It's Time For Love</u>

10. _____The Delfonics   j. <u>After the Love Is Gone</u>

CHARMING CROONERS

A
N
S
W
E
R
S

1.   c. <u>There's Nothing Better Than Love</u>

2.   f. <u>Love Train</u>

3.   i. <u>Don't Say Goodnight – It's Time For Love</u>

4.   e. <u>You'll Never Find Another Love Like Mine</u>

5.   j. <u>After the Love Is Gone</u>

6.   g. <u>Love T.K.O</u>

7.   b. <u>Can't Get Enough Of Your Love</u>

8.   h. <u>Love and Happiness</u>

9.   a. <u>Sweet Love</u>

10.   d. <u>Hey Love</u>

DIVINE DIVAS

Over the years these women have sung songs that have brought couples together.

Match the correct lady with her famous love song.

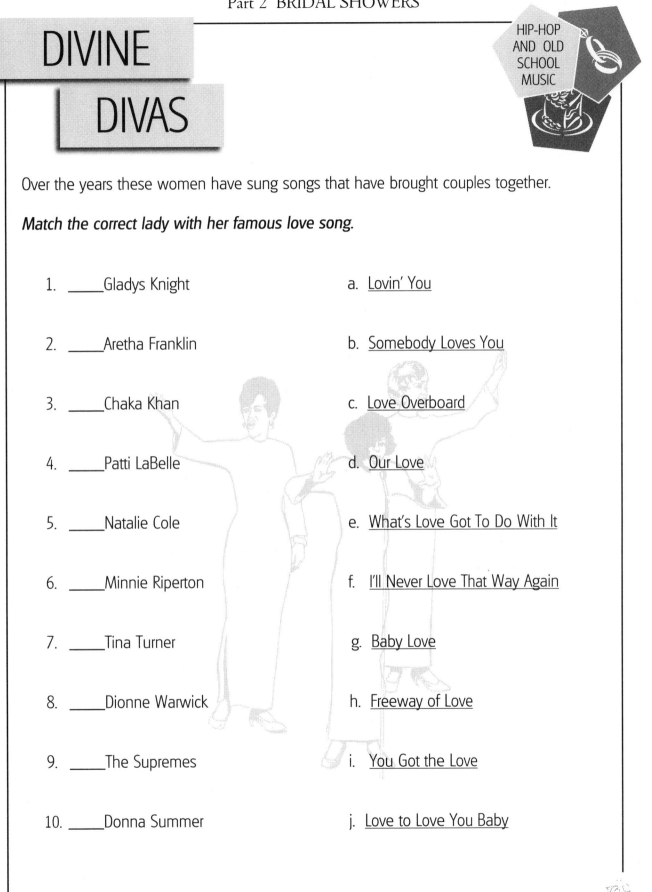

1. _____Gladys Knight

2. _____Aretha Franklin

3. _____Chaka Khan

4. _____Patti LaBelle

5. _____Natalie Cole

6. _____Minnie Riperton

7. _____Tina Turner

8. _____Dionne Warwick

9. _____The Supremes

10. _____Donna Summer

a. <u>Lovin' You</u>

b. <u>Somebody Loves You</u>

c. <u>Love Overboard</u>

d. <u>Our Love</u>

e. <u>What's Love Got To Do With It</u>

f. <u>I'll Never Love That Way Again</u>

g. <u>Baby Love</u>

h. <u>Freeway of Love</u>

i. <u>You Got the Love</u>

j. <u>Love to Love You Baby</u>

DIVINE

DIVAS

A
N
S
W
E
R
S

1. c. <u>Love Overboard</u>
2. h. <u>Freeway of Love</u>
3. i. <u>You Got the Love</u>
4. b. <u>Somebody Loves You</u>
5. d. <u>Our Love</u>
6. a. <u>Lovin' You</u>
7. e. <u>What's Love Got To Do With It</u>
8. f. <u>I'll Never Love That Way Again</u>
9. g. <u>Baby Love</u>
10. j. <u>Love to Love You Baby</u>

MACHO MUSICIANS

HIP-HOP AND OLD SCHOOL MUSIC

These songs, which express love and passion, have been dedicated to women and men of all ages.

Match your favorite musician or musical group with their hit love song.

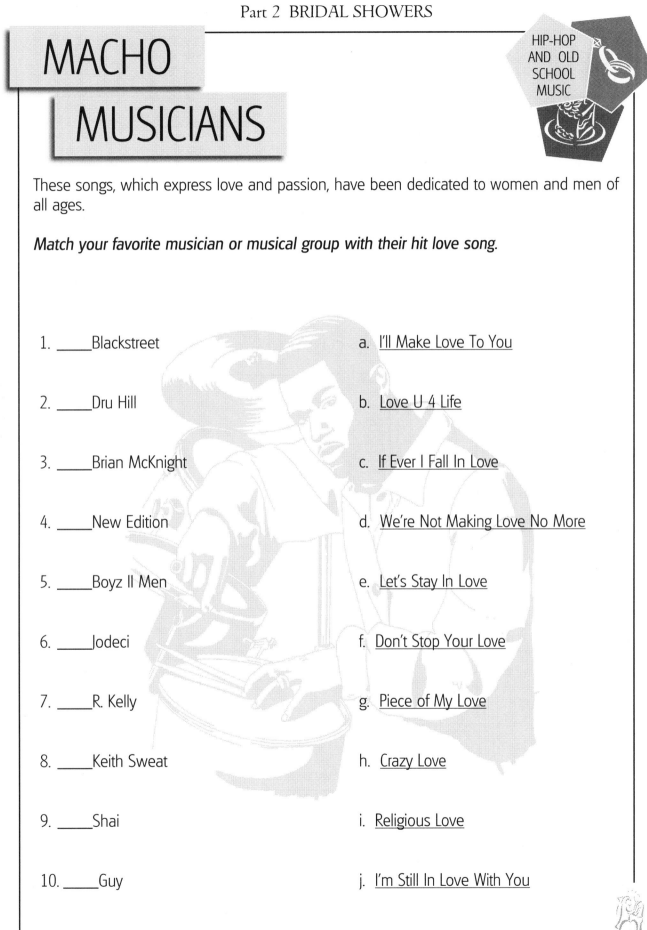

1. _____Blackstreet

2. _____Dru Hill

3. _____Brian McKnight

4. _____New Edition

5. _____Boyz II Men

6. _____Jodeci

7. _____R. Kelly

8. _____Keith Sweat

9. _____Shai

10. _____Guy

a. I'll Make Love To You

b. Love U 4 Life

c. If Ever I Fall In Love

d. We're Not Making Love No More

e. Let's Stay In Love

f. Don't Stop Your Love

g. Piece of My Love

h. Crazy Love

i. Religious Love

j. I'm Still In Love With You

MACHO
MUSICIANS

ANSWERS

1. e. <u>Let's Stay In Love</u>

2. d. <u>We're Not Making Love No More</u>

3. h. <u>Crazy Love</u>

4. j. <u>I'm Still In Love With You</u>

5. a. <u>I'll Make Love To You</u>

6. b. <u>Love U 4 Life</u>

7. i. <u>Religious Love</u>

8. f. <u>Don't Stop Your Love</u>

9. c. <u>If Ever I Fall In Love</u>

10. g. <u>Piece of My Love</u>

SMOOTH SOUNDS

HIP-HOP AND OLD SCHOOL MUSIC

Love can be expressed in many ways. These duets are popular tunes that celebrate a little romance in the world.

Match each pair to their popular tune.

1. _____Diana Ross and Lionel Ritchie   a. Baby Come To Me

2. _____Peabo Bryson and Regina Belle   b. Fire and Desire

3. _____Nat King and Natalie Cole   c. Endless Love

4. _____Rick James and Teena Marie   d. You're All I Need To Get By

5. _____Vanessa Williams and Brian McKnight   e. Unforgettable

6. _____Peaches and Herb   f. A Whole New World

7. _____Michael Jackson and Siedah Garrett   g. I Just Can't Stop Loving You

8. _____Patti Austin and James Ingram   h. Tonight I Celebrate My Love

9. _____Marvin Gaye and Tammi Terrell   i. Love Is

10. _____Roberta Flack and Donny Hathaway   j. Reunited

SMOOTH SOUNDS

ANSWERS

1. c. <u>Endless Love</u>
2. f. <u>A Whole New World</u>
3. e. <u>Unforgettable</u>
4. b. <u>Fire and Desire</u>
5. i. <u>Love Is</u>
6. j. <u>Reunited</u>
7. g. <u>I Just Can't Stop Loving You</u>
8. a. <u>Baby Come to Me</u>
9. d. <u>You're All I Need To Get By</u>
10. h. <u>Tonight I Celebrate My Love</u>

SOULFUL SIRENS

These Ladies of Soul are responsible for several songs that bring couples together.

Match the correct vocalist to her hit "love" song.

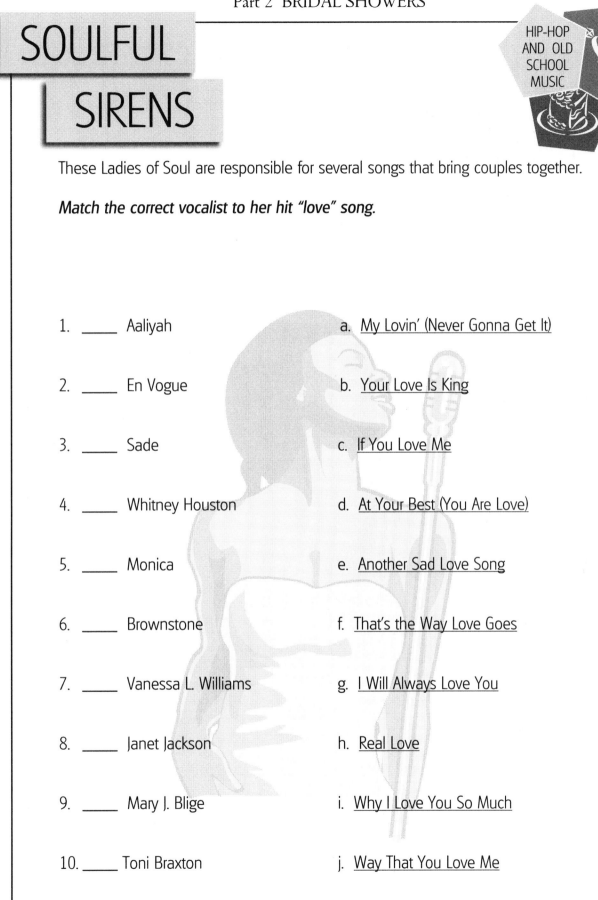

1. _____ Aaliyah

2. _____ En Vogue

3. _____ Sade

4. _____ Whitney Houston

5. _____ Monica

6. _____ Brownstone

7. _____ Vanessa L. Williams

8. _____ Janet Jackson

9. _____ Mary J. Blige

10. _____ Toni Braxton

a. My Lovin' (Never Gonna Get It)

b. Your Love Is King

c. If You Love Me

d. At Your Best (You Are Love)

e. Another Sad Love Song

f. That's the Way Love Goes

g. I Will Always Love You

h. Real Love

i. Why I Love You So Much

j. Way That You Love Me

SOULFUL
SIRENS

A N S W E R S

1. d. <u>At Your Best (You Are Love)</u>
2. a. <u>My Lovin' (Never Gonna Get It)</u>
3. b. <u>You're Love Is King</u>
4. g. <u>I Will Always Love You</u>
5. i. <u>Why I Love You So Much</u>
6. c. <u>If You Love Me</u>
7. j. <u>Way That You Love Me</u>
8. f. <u>That's The Way Love Goes</u>
9. h. <u>Real Love</u>
10. e. <u>Another Sad Love Song</u>

AWESOME ATHLETES

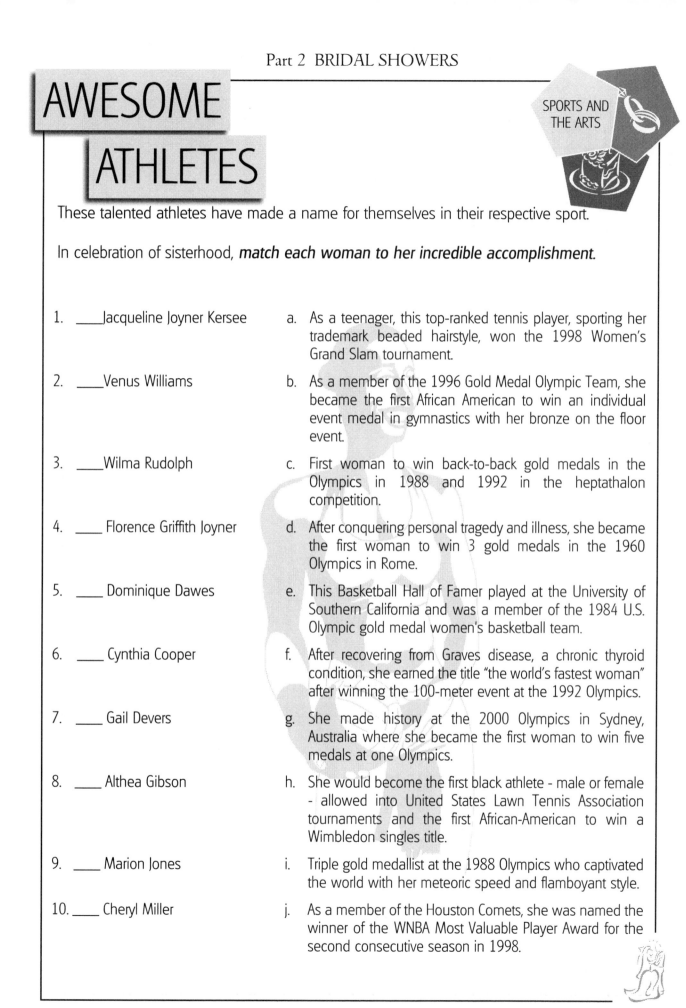

These talented athletes have made a name for themselves in their respective sport.

In celebration of sisterhood, **match each woman to her incredible accomplishment.**

1. ____ Jacqueline Joyner Kersee

    a. As a teenager, this top-ranked tennis player, sporting her trademark beaded hairstyle, won the 1998 Women's Grand Slam tournament.

2. ____ Venus Williams

    b. As a member of the 1996 Gold Medal Olympic Team, she became the first African American to win an individual event medal in gymnastics with her bronze on the floor event.

3. ____ Wilma Rudolph

    c. First woman to win back-to-back gold medals in the Olympics in 1988 and 1992 in the heptathalon competition.

4. ____ Florence Griffith Joyner

    d. After conquering personal tragedy and illness, she became the first woman to win 3 gold medals in the 1960 Olympics in Rome.

5. ____ Dominique Dawes

    e. This Basketball Hall of Famer played at the University of Southern California and was a member of the 1984 U.S. Olympic gold medal women's basketball team.

6. ____ Cynthia Cooper

    f. After recovering from Graves disease, a chronic thyroid condition, she earned the title "the world's fastest woman" after winning the 100-meter event at the 1992 Olympics.

7. ____ Gail Devers

    g. She made history at the 2000 Olympics in Sydney, Australia where she became the first woman to win five medals at one Olympics.

8. ____ Althea Gibson

    h. She would become the first black athlete - male or female - allowed into United States Lawn Tennis Association tournaments and the first African-American to win a Wimbledon singles title.

9. ____ Marion Jones

    i. Triple gold medallist at the 1988 Olympics who captivated the world with her meteoric speed and flamboyant style.

10. ____ Cheryl Miller

    j. As a member of the Houston Comets, she was named the winner of the WNBA Most Valuable Player Award for the second consecutive season in 1998.

AWESOME
ATHLETES

A
N
S
W
E
R
S

1. c. Jacqueline Joyner Kersee
2. a. Venus Williams
3. d. Wilma Rudolph
4. i. Florence Griffith Joyner
5. b. Dominique Dawes
6. j. Cynthia Cooper
7. f. Gail Devers
8. h. Althea Gibson
9. g. Marion Jones
10. e. Cheryl Miller

CAPTURING CREATIVITY

SPORTS AND THE ARTS

With their creative ideas, talents and skills these women have been able to project positive images of African American women in the Arts and Literature.

Match each woman to her notable accomplishment.

1. ____Alice Walker

   a. The first African-American singer to perform with the Metropolitan Opera.

2. ____Dorothy Dandridge

   b. She received the Pulitzer Prize for fiction for her novel The Color Purple.

3. ____Ella Fitzgerald

   c. She is best known for her play, A Raisin in the Sun, which was the first black play produced on Broadway. This drama was about the dreams of a black family seeking a better life.

4. ____ Josephine Baker

   d. Her lyrical soprano voice and unique artistry have captivated audiences around the world, making her one of the most internationally, acclaimed opera singers of our time.

5. ____ Kathleen Battle

   e. 1996 Grammy Award winner for the poem Phenomenal Woman.

6. ____ Lorraine Hansberry

   f. She became known for her famous scat singing style. This songstress is favorably known by the jazz world as the "First Lady of Song."

7. ____ Marion Anderson

   g. This Nobel Prize winner is the author of the bestsellers The Bluest Eye and Tar Baby.

8. ____ Maya Angelou

   h. Some of the titles from this popular author's novels about contemporary black women include Waiting to Exhale, Mama, and How Stella Got Her Groove Back.

9. ____ Terry McMilllan

   i. In Paris in 1925, she starred in La Revue Negre, where her exotic, kinetic stage presence, lithe figure, and cooing vocal style earned her rave reviews and sold-out houses.

10. ____ Toni Morrison

    j. She was the first recognized African American actress and sex symbol, she starred in such movies as Carmen Jones and Porgy and Bess.

CAPTURING
CREATIVITY

A
N
S
W
E
R
S

1. b. Alice Walker
2. j. Dorothy Dandridge
3. f. Ella Fitzgerald
4. i. Josephine Baker
5. d. Kathleen Battle
6. c. Lorraine Hansberry
7. a. Marion Anderson
8. e. Maya Angelou
9. h. Terry Mc Millan
10. g. Toni Morrison

DUELING DUOS

TELEVISION AND MOVIES

Love, deception, humor and trickery are some words that describe the plots in the following movies.

Match the movie titles with their lead actors and actresses.

1. ____ Ali   a. Nicole Ari Parker and Denzel Washington

2. ____ Jason's Lyric   b. Denzel Washington and Kimberly Elise

3. ____ The Nutty Professor II   c. Will Smith and Jada Pinkett Smith

4. ____ John Q   d. Morris Chestnut and Monica Calhoun

5. ____ Mo' Better Blues   e. Alfre Woodard and Delroy Lindo

6. ____ Boomerang   f. Angela Bassett and Denzel Washington

7. ____ Crooklyn   g. Janet Jackson and Eddie Murphy

8. ____ The Best Man   h. Allen Payne and Jada Pinkett Smith

9. ____ Remember the Titans   i. Joia Lee and Denzel Washington

10. ____ Malcolm X   j. Eddie Murphy and Halle Berry

DUELING DUOS

A
N
S
W
E
R
S

1. c. Will Smith and Jada Pinkett Smith
2. h. Allen Payne and Jada Pinkett Smith
3. g. Janet Jackson and Eddie Murphy
4. b. Denzel Washington and Kimberly Elise
5. i. Joia Lee and Denzel Washington
6. j. Eddie Murphy and Halle Berry
7. e. Alfre Woodard and Delroy Lindo
8. d. Morris Chestnut and Monica Calhoun
9. a. Nicole Ari Parker and Denzel Washington
10. f. Angela Bassett and Denzel Washington

MOVIE
MOMENTS

TELEVISION
AND MOVIES

These couples from some of your favorite movies demonstrated that even through heartbreak and disappointment, love prevails.

Given the names of the actual actors and actresses, identify what movies they've appeared together.

1. _____Nia Long and Larenz Tate

2. _____Billy Dee Williams and Diana Ross

3. _____Jada Pinkett Smith and Allen Payne

4. _____Denzel Washington and Joia Lee

5. _____Eddie Murphy and Halle Berry

6. _____Regina King and Cuba Gooding, Jr.

7. _____Nia Long and Mekhi Phifer

8. _____Theresa Randle and Wesley Snipes

9. _____Whitney Houston and Courtney B. Vance

10. _____Halle Berry and Joseph C. Phillips

a. Boomerang

b. Jerry McGuire

c. Soul Food

d. Love Jones

e. Jason's Lyric

f. Mahogany

g. The Preacher's Wife

h. Mo' Better Blues

i. Strictly Business

j. Sugar Hill

MOVIE

MOMENTS

A
N
S
W
E
R
S

1. d. <u>Love Jones</u>
2. f. <u>Mahogany</u>
3. e. <u>Jason's Lyric</u>
4 h. <u>Mo' Better Blues</u>
5. a. <u>Boomerang</u>
6. b. <u>Jerry McGuire</u>
7. c. <u>Soul Food</u>
8. j. <u>Sugar Hill</u>
9. g. <u>The Preacher's Wife</u>
10. i. <u>Strictly Business</u>

TELEVISION

TWOSOMES I

TELEVISION
AND MOVIES

Using their actual character names, *identify these popular African American married couples found on some of your favorite television shows.* See how well you can remember both the first and last names of the characters they've portrayed.

1. Good Times _____
   (Hint: J.J., Thelma, and Michael were their television children.)

2. The Cosby Show _____
   (Hint: He was a doctor and she was a lawyer who together had five children.)

3. The Jeffersons _____
   (Hint: They moved on up...to a deluxe apartment in the sky.)

4. Moesha _____
   (Hint: She is a former Dreamgirl. His character owns a Saturn dealership.)

5. Fresh Prince of Bel Air _____
   (Hint: Carlton, Ashley, and Hillary were their television children, Will was their nephew.)

6. Family Matters _____
   (Hint: Steve Urkel was their pesky television neighbor.)

7. Amen _____
   (Hint: On this show, he played a Reverend, her father used to play the role of George on The Jeffersons)

8. A Different World _____
   (Hint: They both graduated from the fictional "Hillman College".)

9. Living Single _____
   (Hint: He worked as a handyman in her building while she worked at "Flava" magazine.)

10. Martin _____
    (Hint: Her television best friend was Pam, his were Tommy and Cole.)

TELEVISION TWOSOMES I

A
N
S
W
E
R
S

1. James and Florida Evans
2. Cliff and Claire Huxtable
3. George and Louise Jefferson
4. Frank and Dee Mitchell
5. Phillip and Vivian Banks
6. Carl and Hariette Winslow
7. Ruben and Thelma Gregory
8. Dwayne Wayne and Whitley Gilbert Wayne
9. Overton and Sinclair James
10. Martin and Gina Payne

TELEVISION TWOSOMES II

Identify these popular African American married couples found on some of your favorite television shows by last name.

1. For Your Love – Mel and Melina _____

   (Hint: Holly Robinson Peete played the role of a newlywed.)

2. The Bernie Mac Show - Bernie and Wanda _____

   (Hint: One of the original "Kings of Comedy" is raising his sister's three kids.)

3. The Parent 'Hood - Robert and Jerri _____

   (Hint: This 1995 Sitcom starred Robert Townsend and Suzanne Douglass.)

4. The Hughleys - Darryl and Yvonne_____

   (Hint: He is a "King of Comedy"; on this show they have two children, Sydney and Michael.)

5. My Wife and Kids - Michael and Jay_____

   (Hint: A former "In Living Color" star is married to the actress who starred in "Martin".)

6. The Tracy Morgan Show - Tracy and Alicia _____

   (Hint: She is a full-time Mom; he owns a garage. They share a small apartment with their two boys.)

7. The Proud Family – Oscar and Trudy_____

   (Hint: This cartoon husband and wife have three children: Bebe, Cece and Penny.)

8. The Jamie Foxx Show - Helen and Junior _____

   (Hint: Jamie worked for his aunt and uncle who owned the King Towers.)

9. All About The Andersons - Joe and Flo _____

   (Hint: Anthony Anderson moves back into his parents' house with his 8-year-old son.)

10. The Steve Harvey Show – Cedric and and Lovita _____

    (Hint: This couple worked at Booker T. High; he as a gym teacher and she as an administrative assistant.)

TELEVISION
TWOSOMES II

A
N
S
W
E
R
S

1. Mel and Malina Ellis
2. Bernie and Wanda McCullough
3. Robert and Jerri Peterson
4. Darryl and Yvonne Hughley
5. Michael and Jay Kyle
6. Tracy and Alicia Mitchell
7. Oscar and Trudy Proud
8. Helen and Junior King
9. Joe and Flo Anderson
10. Cedric "Jackie" Robinson and Lovita "Alize" Jenkins-Robinson

TELEVISION AND MOVIES

Some of Hollywood's finest have graced the big screen in the following movies.

Match the titles of each movie with its associated lead actors and actresses.

1. ____ Love and Basketball

2. ____ Brown Sugar

3. ____ Two Can Play That Game

4. ____ The Brothers

5. ____ Independence Day

6. ____ Enemy of the State

7. ____ A Thin Line Between Love and Hate

8. ____ Higher Learning

9. ____ In Too Deep

10. ____ How Stella Got Her Groove Back

a. Morris Chestnut and Gabrielle Union

b. Omar Epps and Nia Long

c. Morris Chestnut and Vivica A. Fox

d. Taye Diggs and Angela Bassett

e. Omar Epps and Tyra Banks

f. Will Smith and Regina King

g. Omar Epps and Sanaa Latham

h. Martin Lawrence and Lynn Whitfield

i. Taye Diggs and Sanaa Latham

j. Will Smith and Vivica A. Fox

THEATER
TWOSOMES I

ANSWERS

1. g. Omar Epps and Sanaa Latham
2. i. Taye Diggs and Sanaa Latham
3. c. Morris Chestnut and Vivica A. Fox
4. a. Morris Chestnut and Gabrielle Union
5. j. Will Smith and Vivica A. Fox
6. f. Will Smith and Regina King
7. h. Martin Lawrence and Lynn Whitfield
8. e. Omar Epps and Tyra Banks
9. b. Omar Epps and Nia Long
10. d. Taye Diggs and Angela Bassett

THEATER

TWOSOMES II

Many hip-hop artists have joined the ranks of Hollywood movie stars.

Match the titles of each movie with its associated lead actors and actresses.

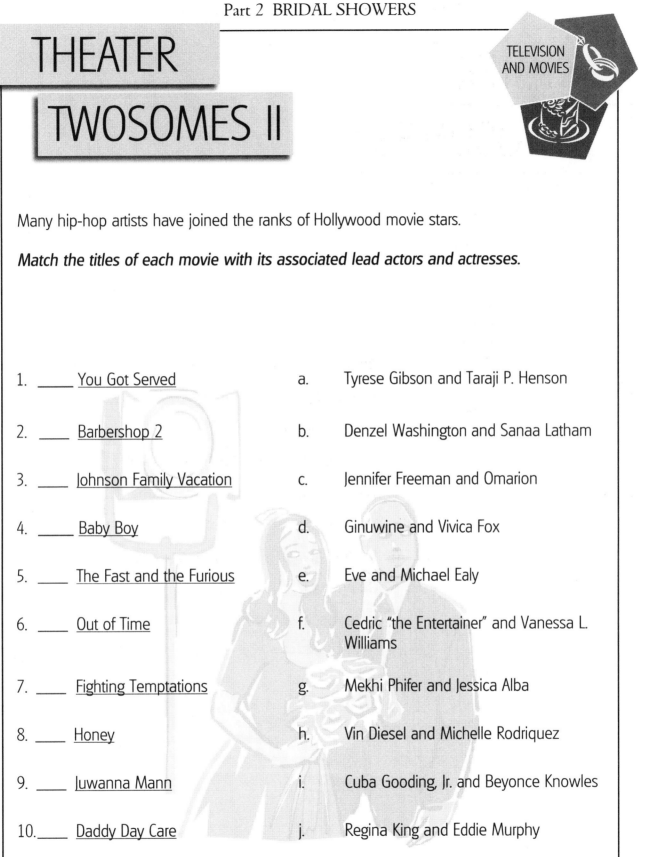

1. _____ You Got Served

2. _____ Barbershop 2

3. _____ Johnson Family Vacation

4. _____ Baby Boy

5. _____ The Fast and the Furious

6. _____ Out of Time

7. _____ Fighting Temptations

8. _____ Honey

9. _____ Juwanna Mann

10._____ Daddy Day Care

a. Tyrese Gibson and Taraji P. Henson

b. Denzel Washington and Sanaa Latham

c. Jennifer Freeman and Omarion

d. Ginuwine and Vivica Fox

e. Eve and Michael Ealy

f. Cedric "the Entertainer" and Vanessa L. Williams

g. Mekhi Phifer and Jessica Alba

h. Vin Diesel and Michelle Rodriquez

i. Cuba Gooding, Jr. and Beyonce Knowles

j. Regina King and Eddie Murphy

THEATER
TWOSOMES II

ANSWERS

1. c. Jennifer Freeman and Omarion (Omari Ishmael Grandbery)
2. e. Eve and Michael Ealy
3. f. Cedric "the Entertainer" and Vanessa L. Williams
4. a. Tyrese Gibson, Taraji P. Henson and Tamara Bass
5. h. Vin Diesel and Michelle Rodriquez
6. b. Denzel Washington and Sanaa Latham
7. i. Cuba Gooding, Jr. and Beyonce Knowles
8. g. Mekhi Phifer and Jessica Alba
9. d. Ginuwine and Vivica Fox
10. j. Regina King and Eddie Murphy

THEATER

TWOSOMES III

TELEVISION
AND MOVIES

Many musical artists have created a second career as Hollywood movie stars.

Match the titles of the movies with its associated lead actors and actresses.

1. ____ Never Die Alone   a. Derek Luke and Meagan Good

2. ____ Save The Last Dance   b. Derek Luke and Joy Bryant

3. ____ Biker Boys   c. Reagan Gomez-Preston and DMX

4. ____ Antwone Fisher   d. Julia Stiles and Sean Patrick Thomas

5. ____ Bad Boyz II   e. Jet Li and Aaliyah

6. ____ All About the Benjamins   f. Mekhi Phifer and Julia Stiles

7. ____ Romeo Must Die   g. Gabrielle Union and Will Smith

8. ____ Big Momma's House   h. L.L. Cool J and Vivica A. Fox

9. ____ O   i. Eva Mendes and Mike Epps

10. ____ Kingdom Come   j. Martin Lawrence and Nia Long

THEATER TWOSOMES III

ANSWERS

1. c. Reagan Gomez-Preston and DMX
2. d. Julia Stiles and Sean Patrick Thomas
3. a. Derek Luke and Meagan Good
4. b. Derek Luke and Joy Bryant
5. g. Gabrielle Union and Will Smith
6. i. Eva Mendes and Mike Epps
7. e. Jet Li and Aaliyah
8. j. Martin Lawrence and Nia Long
9. f. Mekhi Phifer and Julia Stiles
10. h. L.L. Cool J and Vivica A. Fox

ANNIVERSARY GIFTS

Once married the happy couple will continue to celebrate their love through anniversaries.

Match each anniversary with it's traditional gift.

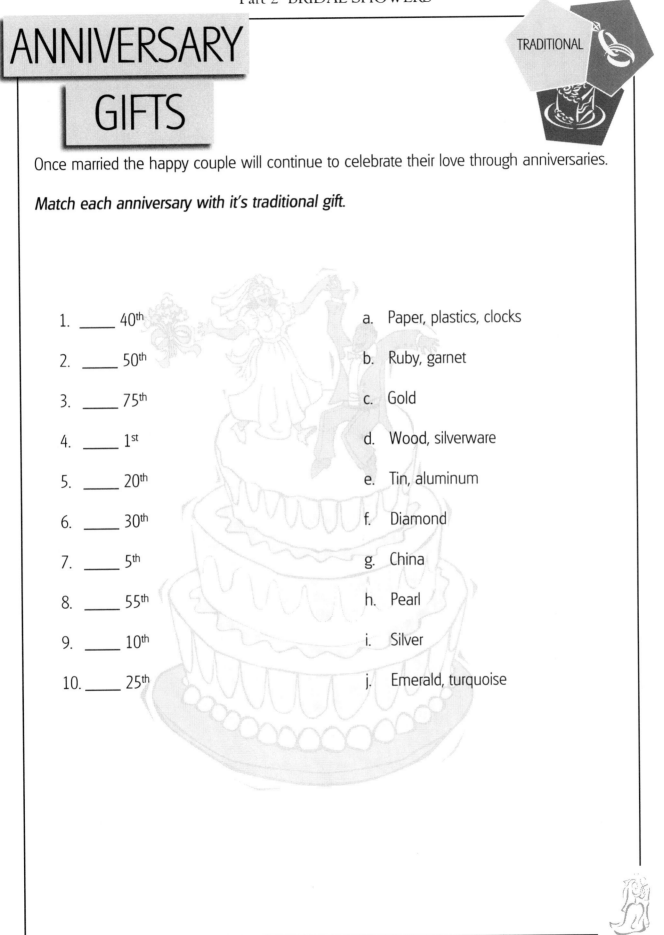

1. _____ 40th   a. Paper, plastics, clocks

2. _____ 50th   b. Ruby, garnet

3. _____ 75th   c. Gold

4. _____ 1st   d. Wood, silverware

5. _____ 20th   e. Tin, aluminum

6. _____ 30th   f. Diamond

7. _____ 5th   g. China

8. _____ 55th   h. Pearl

9. _____ 10th   i. Silver

10. _____ 25th   j. Emerald, turquoise

ANNIVERSARY GIFTS

ANSWERS

1.   b. Ruby, garnet
2.   c. Gold
3.   f. Diamond
4.   a. Paper, plastics, clocks
5.   g. China
6.   h. Pearl
7.   d. Wood, silverware
8.   j. Emerald, turquoise
9.   e. Tin, aluminum
10.   i. Silver

BRIDAL
BRAIN
TEASER

TRADITIONAL

See how many pictures you can memorize.

Study the pictures for 30 seconds then turn over the paper and list as many of the objects you can remember.

BRIDAL
BRAIN
TEASER

_____

_____

_____

_____

_____

_____

_____

_____

BRIDAL MYSTERY

TRADITIONAL

How well do you know the bride? *Answer these ten questions.*

Compare your answers to the guest-of-honor as she answers these mystery questions during the shower.

1. Birthday _____

2. Number of brothers and sisters _____

3. Shoe size _____

4. Honeymoon location _____

5. Wedding date _____

6. Favorite food _____

7. Year graduated from high school _____

8. Wedding colors _____

9. Birthplace _____

10. Job title _____

EXHAUSTING ESCAPADE

TRADITIONAL

This mother and daughter have been in search of the perfect wedding dress for more than five hours and have decided to take a break.

Unscramble the wedding related items then use the letters in the circles to solve the final puzzle. Clue: The final puzzle is something that is now on the top of their priority list..

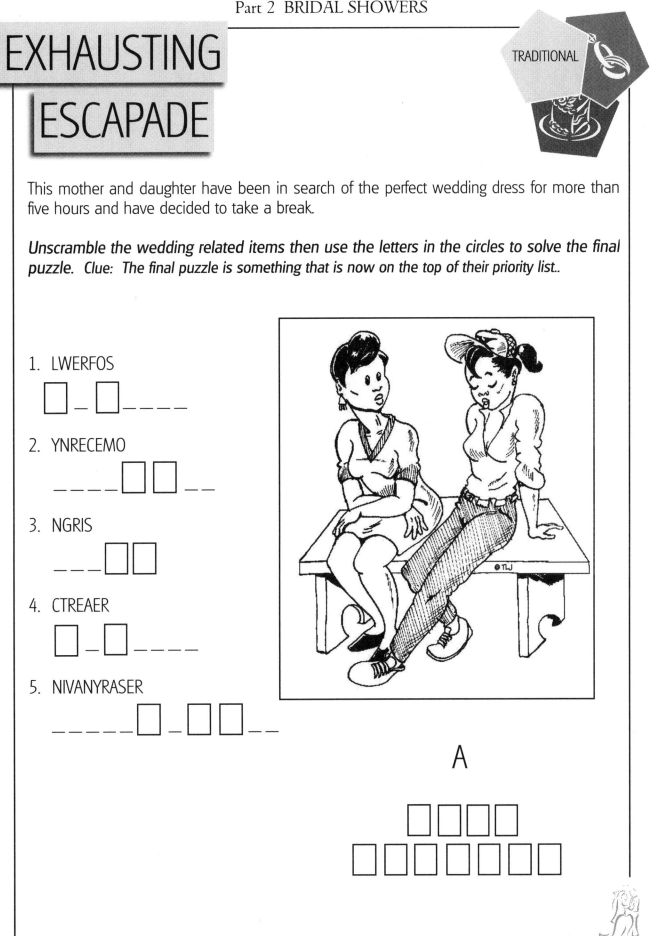

1. LWERFOS

☐ _ ☐ _ _ _ _

2. YNRECEMO

_ _ _ _ _ ☐ ☐ _ _

3. NGRIS

_ _ _ ☐ ☐

4. CTREAER

☐ _ ☐ _ _ _ _

5. NIVANYRASER

_ _ _ _ _ _ ☐ _ ☐ ☐ _ _

A

☐ ☐ ☐ ☐
☐ ☐ ☐ ☐ ☐ ☐

EXHAUSTING ESCAPADE

ANSWERS

1. FLOWERS
2. CEREMONY
3. RINGS
4. CATERER
5. ANNIVERSARY

A FOOT MASSAGE

FINANCIAL FIASCO

TRADITIONAL

After spending 3 hours adding up estimates for their dream wedding, find out what the newlyweds were thinking. Unscramble the wedding related items and use the letters in the circles to solve the final puzzle.

1. RCEPENIOT

   _ _ _ _ ☐ _ _ _ _

2. MILSIUONE

   _ _ _ ☐ _ _ _ _ _

3. XEDUTO

   _ _ _ ☐ _ _

4. VLEI

   _ ☐ _ _

5. SRELOWF

   _ ☐ _ _ _ _ _

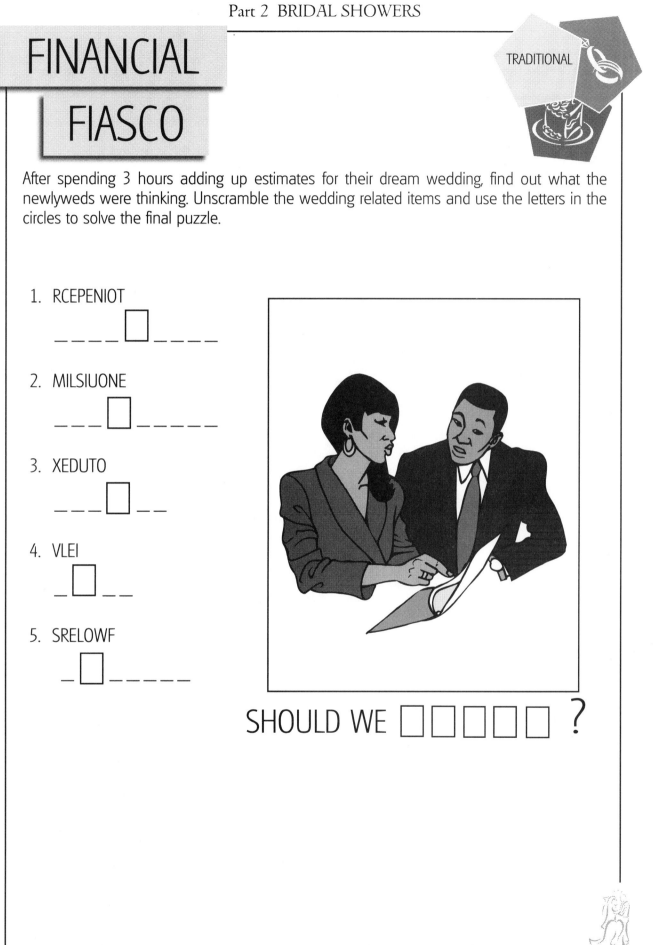

SHOULD WE ☐☐☐☐☐ ?

FINANCIAL FIASCO

A
N
S
W
E
R
S

1. RECEPTION
2. LIMOUSINE
3. TUXEDO
4. VEIL
5. FLOWERS

SHOULD WE ELOPE?

GROOM'S
GAME 1

TRADITIONAL

Prior to the shower, ask the groom these questions.

At the shower, have each guest complete the questions as well. The guest who has the most answers matching the groom's answers wins.

1. What's the groom's favorite food? _____

2. What year did he graduate from high school? _____

3. How old was he when he got his first kiss? _____

4. Where did the bride and groom go on their first date together? _____

5. What size shoe does he wear? _____

6. What's the groom's favorite cologne? _____

7. What age did he receive his driver's license? _____

8. What animal would the groom compare the bride to? _____

9. What would the groom consider the bride's best feature? _____

10. Who is the groom's favorite sports team? _____

11. Who is his favorite actress? _____

12. What sport(s) did he play in high school? _____

13. Who was his favorite elementary school teacher? _____

14. Who taught the groom to tie his shoes? _____

15. What was the name of his first pet? _____

GROOM'S
GAME II

Prior to the shower ask the groom these questions.

At the shower, have each guest complete the questions as well. The guest who has the most answers matching the groom's answers wins.

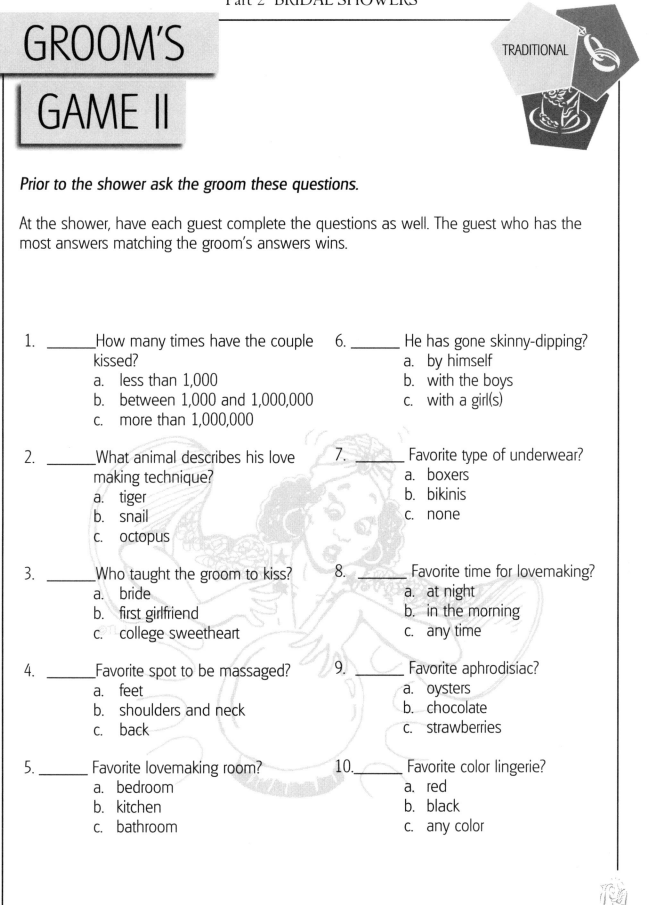

1. _____ How many times have the couple kissed?
   a. less than 1,000
   b. between 1,000 and 1,000,000
   c. more than 1,000,000

2. _____ What animal describes his love making technique?
   a. tiger
   b. snail
   c. octopus

3. _____ Who taught the groom to kiss?
   a. bride
   b. first girlfriend
   c. college sweetheart

4. _____ Favorite spot to be massaged?
   a. feet
   b. shoulders and neck
   c. back

5. _____ Favorite lovemaking room?
   a. bedroom
   b. kitchen
   c. bathroom

6. _____ He has gone skinny-dipping?
   a. by himself
   b. with the boys
   c. with a girl(s)

7. _____ Favorite type of underwear?
   a. boxers
   b. bikinis
   c. none

8. _____ Favorite time for lovemaking?
   a. at night
   b. in the morning
   c. any time

9. _____ Favorite aphrodisiac?
   a. oysters
   b. chocolate
   c. strawberries

10. _____ Favorite color lingerie?
   a. red
   b. black
   c. any color

MARITAL
MADNESS

TRADITIONAL

Unscramble the essential elements of a successful relationship.

1. TMENMIOCM _____

2. YHTONES _____

3. TURST _____

4. REPCEST _____

5. TIEPAENC _____

6. CATIONMUNICMO _____

7. VOLE _____

8. MORHU _____

9. MENTEXCITE _____

10. FIDENCONCE _____

11. THAIF _____

12. SFLE TSEEME _____

13. ITDFIELY _____

14. DMIETERNAONTI _____

15. SICACRIFE _____

16. ROCEMAN _____

17. PACOMILTIBITY _____

18. SNGHRIA _____

19. CMISOMPROE _____

20. INATIMCY _____

MARITAL

MADNESS

ANSWERS

1. COMMITMENT
2. HONESTY
3. TRUST
4. RESPECT
5. PATIENCE
6. COMMUNICATION
7. LOVE
8. HUMOR
9. EXCITEMENT
10. CONFIDENCE
11. FAITH
12. SELF ESTEEM
13. FIDELITY
14. DETERMINATION
15. SACRIFICE
16. ROMANCE
17. COMPATIBILITY
18. SHARING
19. COMPROMISE
20. INTIMACY

MATRIMONIAL MATCHES I

From the list of well-known African American celebrities, *match the ten (10) married couples.*

While some couples are still married, others have separated and are now married to someone else.

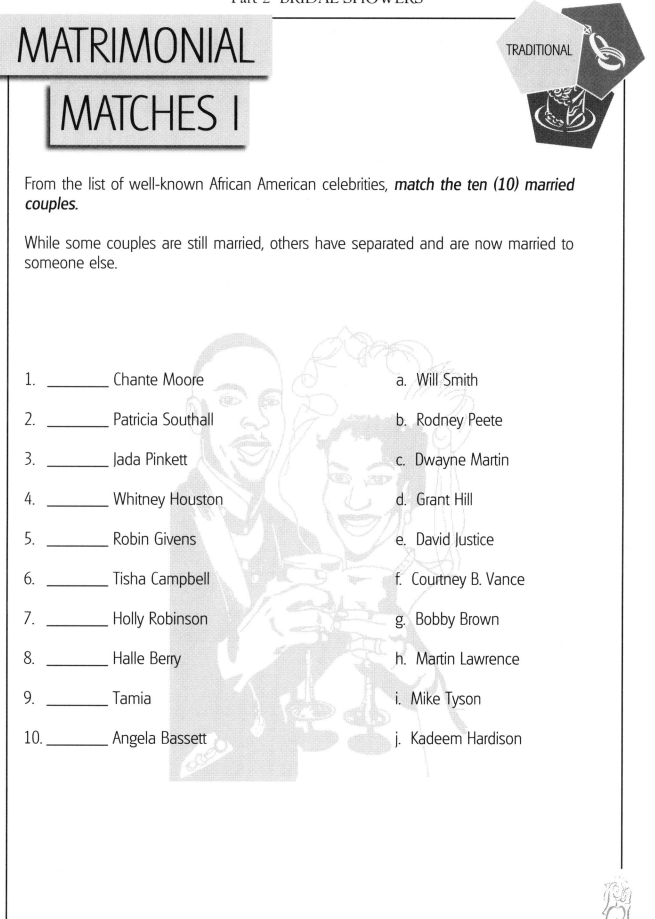

1. _____ Chante Moore   a. Will Smith

2. _____ Patricia Southall   b. Rodney Peete

3. _____ Jada Pinkett   c. Dwayne Martin

4. _____ Whitney Houston   d. Grant Hill

5. _____ Robin Givens   e. David Justice

6. _____ Tisha Campbell   f. Courtney B. Vance

7. _____ Holly Robinson   g. Bobby Brown

8. _____ Halle Berry   h. Martin Lawrence

9. _____ Tamia   i. Mike Tyson

10. _____ Angela Bassett   j. Kadeem Hardison

MATRIMONIAL
MATCHES I

A
N
S
W
E
R
S

1. j. Chante Moore and Kadeem Hardison, married in 1996 and divorced in 2000

2. h. Martin Lawrence and Patricia Southall, married July 1995, divorced January 1997

3. a. Jada Pinkett and Will Smith, married Dec. 1997

4. g. Whitney Houston and Bobby Brown, married July 1992

5. i. Robin Givens and Mike Tyson, after 16 months of marriage they divorced on Valentine's Day, 1989.

6. c. Tisha Campbell and Dwayne Martin

7. b. Rodney Peete and Holly Robinson, married 1995

8. e. David Justice and Halle Berry, married January 1993, divorced June 1997

9. d. Tamia and Grant Hill married in 1999.

10. f. Angela Bassett and Courtney Vance, married October 1997

MATRIMONIAL
MATCHES II

From the list of African American celebrities, *match the ten (10) couples who are or were married.*

1. _____ Solange Knowles

2. _____ Sole

3. _____ Vanessa Laine

4. _____ Mary J. Blige

5. _____ Wyclef Jean

6. _____ Flex Alexander

7. _____ Vanessa L. Williams

8. _____ Chante Moore

9. _____ Jada Pinkett

10. _____ Halle Berry

a. Ginuwine

b. Marie Claudinette

c. Daniel Smith

d. Rick Fox

e. Kobe Bryant

f. Will Smith

g. Kendu Isaacs

h. Eric Benet

i. Kenny Lattimore

j. Shanice Wilson

MATRIMONIAL
MATCHES II

A
N
S
W
E
R
S

1. c. Daniel Smith
2. a. Ginuwine
3. e. Kobe Bryant
4. g. Kendu Isaacs
5. b. Marie Claudinette
6. j. Shanice Wilson
7. d. Rick Fox
8. i. Kenny Lattimore
9. f. Will Smith
10. h. Eric Benet

MATRIMONIAL MEDLEY

TRADITIONAL

Unscramble the following wedding related items.

1. LPROPSAO _____

2. GEGAENTNEM _____

3. TIONSINVATI _____

4. MOUSINLIE _____

5. REDIB _____

6. GMORO _____

7. CUHRCH _____

8. BOEQTUU _____

9. BEARGNIRRE _____

10. WERFLO RGIL _____   _____

11. GRISN _____

12. RGATRE _____

13. PHRAREHPOTOG _____

14. CTAERER _____

15. IVEL _____

16. RAMIAGRE _____

17. WONG _____

18. TXDOUE _____

19. VOSW _____

20. OMONYEHON _____

MATRIMONIAL MEDLEY

ANSWERS

1. PROPOSAL
2. ENGAGEMENT
3. INVITATIONS
4. LIMOUSINE
5. BRIDE
6. GROOM
7. CHURCH
8. BOUQUET
9. RINGBEARER
10. FLOWER GIRL
11. RINGS
12. GARTER
13. PHOTOGRAPHER
14. CATERER
15. VEIL
16. MARRIAGE
17. GOWN
18. TUXEDO
19. VOWS
20. HONEYMOON

MINISTERIAL MISTAKE

This proud minister is right in the middle of performing a wedding when he realizes he's forgotten the most important part of the ceremony.

Unscramble the wedding-related items and use the letters in the circles to solve the final puzzle.

1. XEDUTO

   _ _ _ ☐ _ _

2. MOGOR

   _ _ _ _ ☐

3. LPSAROPO

   _ _ _ _ _ _ ☐ _

4. RSNIG

   _ _ ☐ _ _

5. WOSV

   _ _ _ ☐

THE COUPLE'S ☐☐☐☐☐

MINISTERIAL MISTAKE

ANSWERS

1. TUXEDO
2. GROOM
3. PROPOSAL
4. RINGS
5. VOWS

THE COUPLE'S NAMES

PATIENT
GROOM

TRADITIONAL

After spending hours in a bridal store looking at bridesmaid's dresses, find out what's really on this brother's mind.

Unscramble the wedding related items and use the letters in the circles to solve the final problem and read his thoughts.

1. RLERGIWOLF

   __ __ ⬜ ⬜ __ __ ⬜ __ __ __

2. IVEL

   __ ⬜ __ __

3. SEDIAMDIRB

   __ __ __ __ __ ⬜ __ __ ⬜ __ __

4. PHERARGHOPOT

   __ __ __ __ ⬜ __ __ __ __ ⬜ __ __

5. NLDECA

   ⬜ ⬜ ⬜ ⬜ __ __ __

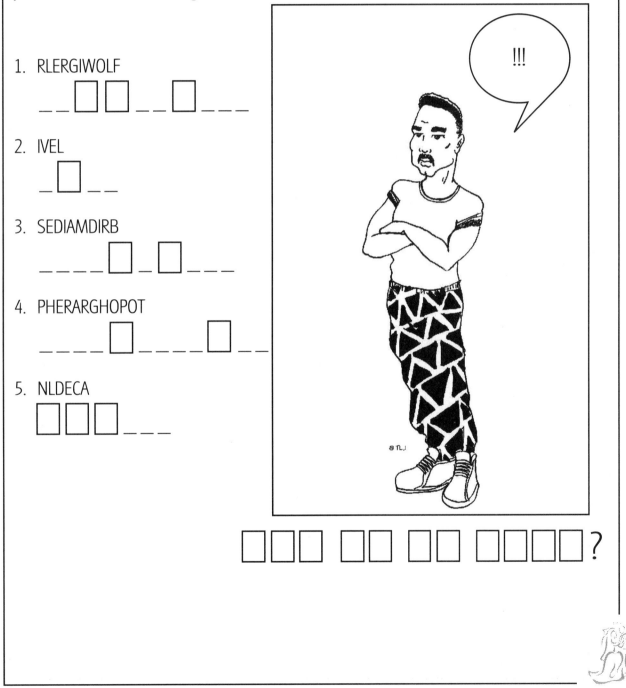

⬜ ⬜ ⬜ ⬜ ⬜ ⬜ ⬜ ⬜ ⬜ ⬜ ?

PATIENT
GROOM

ANSWERS

1. FLOWERGIRL
2. VEIL
3. BRIDESMAID
4. CANDLE
5. PHOTOGRAPHER

CAN WE GO HOME?

RELIABLE REMEDIES

TRADITIONAL

If after getting a cold, "Big Daddy" turns into "Mama's Baby" there are a few things a new bride should know. Some of these unusual remedies for some of life's ailments have been handed down from generation to generation; others have been created especially for this game.

Correctly identify the statements, using "T" for true and "F" for false.

1. _____ Eating Vick's Vapor Rub instead of rubbing it on your chest cures the cold and clears congestion.

2. _____ To soothe the pain of a toothache, rub your gums with peppermint-flavored tea bags.

3. _____ You can reduce the pain of a bee sting with a paste of baking soda and water.

4. _____ Soaking your feet in a mixture of grated ginger and warm water is sure to eliminate foot odor.

5. _____ To reduce the symptoms of a cold and clear sinus passages, ground fresh garlic and place in a small bag. Tie the bag loosely around your throat.

6. _____ Brushing with cayenne pepper will keep your teeth white and cavity-free.

7. _____ To stop a dry cough, sprinkle pillowcase with apple cider vinegar before going to sleep.

8. _____ To eliminate the swelling of a sprained ankle, wrap it in a mixture of Epsom salt and ground pepper.

9. _____ A teaspoon of sugar mixed with three to five drops of turpentine will cure the cold.

10. _____ Drink tea made with the leaves of papaya and coconut trees to eliminate sore joints caused by arthritis.

RELIABLE
REMEDIES

A
N
S
W
E
R
S

1. True
2. False
3. True
4. False
5. True
6. True
7. True
8. False
9. True
10. False

TRADITIONAL CUSTOM

TRADITIONAL

This ancient African wedding custom seen here is still in use today.

Unscramble the wedding related items and use the letters in the circles to solve the final puzzle to name this custom.

1. MEGARIAR

   ☐ _ _ _ _ ☐ _ _ _

2. BEQTOUU

   ☐ _ _ _ _ _ _ ☐

3. RTGEAR

   ☐ _ _ _ _ ☐☐

4. NEHONOYMO

   _ _ _ _ _ ☐☐☐☐

5. JITSUEC FO HET CAPEE

   ☐☐ _ _ _ _ _

   _ _ _ ☐ _

   ☐ _ _ _ _

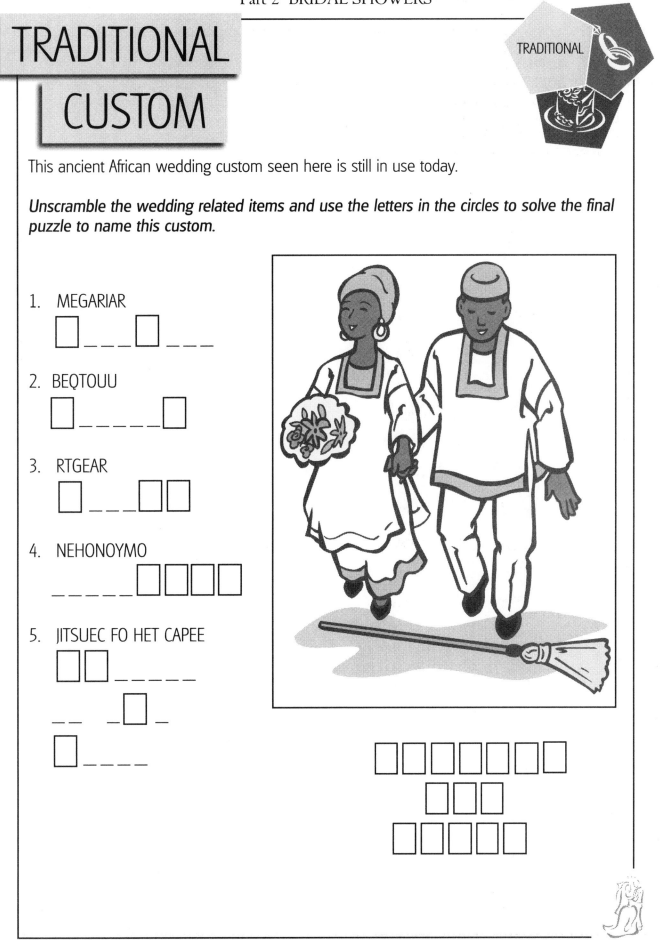

☐☐☐☐☐☐☐

☐☐☐

☐☐☐☐☐

TRADITIONAL
CUSTOM

A
N
S
W
E
R
S

1. MARRIAGE
2. BOUQUET
3. GARTER
4. HONEYMOON
5. JUSTICE OF THE PEACE

JUMPING THE BROOM

TRADITIONAL
TRIVIA I

Test your knowledge of these wedding facts using "T" for true and "F" for false.

1. _____ Wedding rings are traditionally worn on the right hand.

2. _____ A mock bride is usually a young lady dressed in a wedding dress in the bridal party.

3. _____ The bridal party is a celebration held at the home of the bride on the night before the wedding.

4. _____ A runner is normally placed in the aisle of the church before the wedding is started so the guests will keep their shoes clean.

5. _____ To form a receiving line at a wedding, all guests should stand in a straight line and greet the bridal party as they leave the church.

6. _____ Rain on the wedding day is considered lucky.

7. _____ Throwing of rice is a traditional way of wishing the newlyweds many children.

8. _____ The never-ending circle of a wedding band symbolizes eternal love by its lack of a beginning and an end.

9. _____ A groom's cake is a small cake normally accompanying the wedding cake.

10. _____ Pages (or train bearers) are young boys who carry a bride's long train.

TRADITIONAL
TRIVIA I

A
N
S
W
E
R
S

1. False
2. True
3. False
4. False
5. False
6. True
7. True
8. True
9. True
10. True

TRADITIONAL

TRIVIA II

TRADITIONAL

How much do you know about weddings?

Correctly identify the following wedding related facts, using "T" for true and "F" for false.

1. _____ The phrase "something old, something new, something borrowed, something green".

2. _____ On the wedding day, it's "good luck" for the bride and groom to see each other before the wedding.

3. _____ The traditional first-year anniversary gift is paper.

4. _____ Bridal showers occur when it rains the morning of the wedding.

5. _____ The bride's family sits on the left side of the church, while the groom's family sits on the right.

6. _____ "Informals" are cards given to family and friends that announce the upcoming wedding.

7. _____ At the reception, the "receiving line" is where guests stand in line to make a toast to the newlyweds.

8. _____ The "silver" wedding anniversary is celebrated after fifty years of marriage.

9. _____ "Wedding favors" are good deeds done especially for the bride and groom.

10._____ At the altar, the bride stands on the right, groom on the left.

TRADITIONAL
TRIVIA II

ANSWERS

1. False
2. False
3. True
4. False
5. False
6. False
7. False
8. True
9. False
10. True

WEDDING DAY DISTRESS

The best man has just told the groom that he still has one very important thing to do before the wedding.

Unscramble the wedding related items and use the letters in the circles to solve the final puzzle and find out what it is.

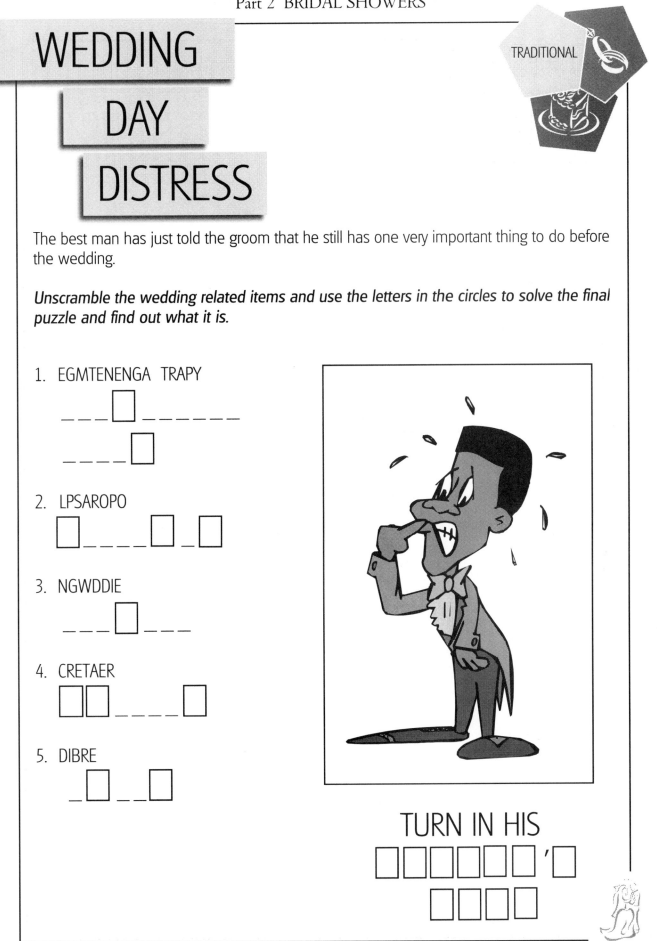

1. EGMTENENGA TRAPY

   _ _ _ ☐ _ _ _ _ _ _ _

   _ _ _ _ _ ☐

2. LPSAROPO

   ☐ _ _ _ _ _ ☐ _ ☐

3. NGWDDIE

   _ _ _ ☐ _ _ _

4. CRETAER

   ☐ ☐ _ _ _ _ ☐

5. DIBRE

   _ ☐ _ _ ☐

TURN IN HIS

☐☐☐☐☐☐ '☐

☐☐☐☐

WEDDING DAY DISTRESS

ANSWERS

1. ENGAGEMENT PARTY
2. PROPOSAL
3. WEDDING
4. CATERER
5. BRIDE

TURN IN HIS PLAYER'S CARD

Part 3
BABY SHOWERS

This section offers themes and games for a variety of baby showers. If your guests are more comfortable at a quiet sit-down event or would rather laugh and talk loudly there are a multitude of ideas included within.

Themes in this section range from to <u>Fill the Nursery</u> where guests are asked to bring the supplies a new mom will need to <u>Time to Spare</u> where guests donate an hour of his or her time for babysitting services.

Traditional games such as charades, musical chairs, and hot potato will make your guests get out of their seats and move their feet. Other games included in this section can be compared to sprinkling brown sugar and cinnamon on candied yams. With titles such as <u>Brown Sugar Brothers and Sisters</u> and <u>Cinnamon Coated Celebrities,</u> these games will make your shower a sugary-sweet event.

Chapter 1
BABY SHOWER THEMES

A to Z

For this type of shower, each guest will be assigned a letter for which they will have to bring an item starting with that same letter. For example, a guest assigned the letter "B" might bring a blanket while a guest assigned an "R" might bring a rattle. Games in the next section that would be appropriate for this theme include <u>Baby Hodgepodge</u>, <u>What's In Mommy's Baby Bag</u>, or <u>Memory Challenge</u>.

Afro-centric Baby Shower

Remove shoes in recognition of the sacredness of the ritual. Pour water from a wooden cup into a plant. Say a prayer to honor the ancestors. This is a common way to begin African ceremonies. The Mother-of-Honor sits in the middle of the circle under a Kente cloth umbrella. Guests go around the sista-circle and share childbirth or child rearing experiences. All stand. Move counter-clockwise around the Mother-of-Honor. Share wisdom while attaching gifts of money (Ghana). Sit in the sista-circle, meditatively sending positive energy to the new mother. Guests share a poem or song. Play soothing music. Rain, ocean or African drum sounds are ideal. Form a trust walk to send your love to the new mother. Blindfold the Mother-of-Honor and form two lines. As she walks through, guests gently touch her. They offer hugs as reminders that "she may not see where she is going but she is going to get there." Sit down again in the sista-circle; each guest gives the Mother-of-Honor a blessing while touching her shoulder. Close with a benediction, eating and opening of the gifts. For a special touch, hire a storyteller and

drummers. Games that correspond with this theme include <u>Labor and Delivery Rituals</u> and <u>Across the Globe</u>.

Around the Clock

For this theme, each guest brings a gift appropriate to his or her assigned time of day. Celebrate every hour starting with baby bottles and bibs which can be used all day, a sterling silver fork and spoon set and high chair to be used during a morning feeding, a stroller to be used at noon when mom and baby go for a walk or a comfortable silk bathrobe to help mom relax in the evening with the baby. Any of the games in the next section would be suited for this type of shower.

Childhood Memories

This is a great event for close friends and family of the expectant mom. Guests are asked to bring old photos of themselves from their childhood or teen years. They should also bring a short anecdote or funny story in writing, recalling the happy times portrayed in the photo. As each person shares their special memory, it is a way for all the guests to get to know each other. <u>Say Cheese!</u> is an excellent game for this shower.

College Tuition Fund

For the couple that wants to start planning for their child's education, guests at this shower will contribute to a college tuition fund. The 529-education savings plan is designed to help families' set-aside funds for future college costs. Another option is the Coverdell Education Savings Account (formally known as the Education IRA), which allows families to save for elementary, and secondary school expenses. Any of the games in the next section would entertain the guests at your shower.

Fashion Extravaganza

When invitations are sent out for this shower, assign each guest a size and type of clothing. Items such as pajamas, one-piece sleepers, undershirts, and bodysuits in various sizes will eliminate duplicative gifts and are sure to be a hit with the new mom. Any of the games in the next section would be suited for this type of shower.

Fill the Nursery

If this is mom's first baby she may need some help filling the nursery. At this shower guests are asked to bring the supplies a new mom will need. Everything from diapers, baby blankets and accessories for the crib will be appropriate for this type of shower. Appropriate games for this type of shower include <u>Baby Hodgepodge</u>, <u>What's In Mommy's Baby Bag</u>, or <u>Memory Challenge</u>.

Musical Medley

For this shower purchase music or books with nursery rhyme lyrics that both the new mom and baby will enjoy. Can you remember the words to <u>Hush little baby</u>, <u>Itsy bitsy spider</u>, or <u>Twinkle, twinkle little star</u>? Sing-along songs on video, DVD or cassette will be appropriate gifts for the baby, as he or she gets older. <u>Baby Song Musical Chairs</u>, <u>Who Said That?</u>, <u>Nursery Numbers</u>, or <u>Colorful Characters</u> are games that would accompany this theme.

Noah's Ark

As the animals boarded Noah's ark in pairs, this type of shower is planned for the arrival of twins. It is quite all right to have two of each item. Although there are no specific games related to this theme any game from the next section would be enjoyed by your guests.

Pampered Princess

This shower is perfect for the mom that's having her second or third child. Since she may already have the necessities that baby needs why not pamper her. Gift certificates for a day at the spa or an individual spa treatment will fit this theme as well. Scented candles and body oils will also help to pamper a new mom. Additionally, comfortable slippers and lounge wear will help the new mom relax once baby arrives.

Season-to-Season

One option for this type of shower is to assign each guest a season for which they will have bring an item that can be used during that time frame. Another option for this type of shower is to pick the opposite season, such as a winter shower during the summer or vice versa. All the gifts should reflect the season, such as shorts, t-shirts or sandals in the middle of January, or a snowsuit, hats or gloves in the heat of July.

The Three R's

This shower theme is all about the three R's, readin', 'ritin and 'rithmetic. Gifts such as activity mats and blocks to play with and on, books to be read by Mom or Dad, and other educational toys will certainly fit this theme. Another gift idea for this type of shower includes educational videos.

Time to Spare

For the mom who may have everything but free time why not give her just that. Create gift certificates that will allow each guest to fill in a task or amount of time that he or she is willing to donate to the guest-of-honor. For example, one guest may donate an hour of his or her time for babysitting services while another guest may choose to contribute grocery-shopping services. When mom needs free time she can cash in one of her certificates. The Gift Certificates in the Resources section could be duplicated, personalized and given to your guests.

NOTES

Chapter 2
BABY SHOWER GAMES

HELPFUL HINT

Prior to the shower select the games you will use for your event. To ensure you have enough copies for each of your guests, make at least 5 extra copies per game. For example, if you expect 20 people to attend, make at least 25 copies per game.

BROWN SUGAR
BROTHERS
AND SISTERS

CELEBRITIES

Using your knowledge of these celebrity siblings, *fill in the blanks* with the names of these brothers and sisters. See if you can identify them by first name.

1. _____ and _____ Knowles
(Hint: These sisters from Texas can sing, act and dance. One starred in Johnson Family Vacation, the other in Austin Powers in Goldmember.)

2. _____ and _____ Gooding
(Hint: These brothers started acting when they were young. The older one starred in The Fighting Temptations, while the younger brother appeared in Baby Boy and Playmakers.

3. _____ and _____ Williams
(Hint: These famous tennis players have won numerous tournaments, including Wimbledon and the U.S. Open.)

4. _____ and _____ Mowry
(Hint: These twin sisters had their own television show, Sister, Sister.)

5. _____ and _____ Rock
(Hint: These comedians have been on television and movies in Head of State, Saturday Night Live, and All of Us.)

6 _____ and _____ Wayans
(Hint: These comedians have had several hit movies including White Chicks and the Scary Movie trilogy.)

7. _____ and _____ Norwood
(Hint: This brother and sister can act, sing, and dance. They have both appeared on television on her show Moesha.)

8. _____ and _____ Jackson
(Hint: This King of Pop and his sister, whose costume malfunctioned at the 2004 Superbowl, are two of the most famous siblings in their family.)

9. _____ and _____ Winans
(Hint: This brother and sister who have performed as a duet are from one of the most famous gospel families.)

10. _____ Grandberry and _____ Houston
(Hint: These brothers can act, sing and dance. Their musical hits include Bump Bump Bump, Uh Huh, and Clubbin'.)

BROWN SUGAR
BROTHERS
AND SISTERS

A
N
S
W
E
R
S

1. Beyonce and Solange Knowles
2. Cuba Jr. and Omar Gooding
3. Venus and Serena Williams
4. Tia and Tamera Mowry
5. Chris and Tony Rock
6. Marlon and Shawn Wayans
7. Brandy and Ray J. Norwood
8. Michael and Janet Jackson
9. Bebe and Cece Winans
10. Omari Ishmael Grandberry (Omarion) and Marcus Houston

CINNAMON-COATED

CELEBRITIES

CELEBRITIES

Will the new baby have as many brothers and sisters as there are in these families?

Fill in the blanks with the names of these celebrity siblings.

WAYANS

WINANS

_____

_____

_____

_____

_____

_____

_____

_____

_____

_____

_____

_____

JACKSONS

_____

_____

_____

_____

_____

_____

_____

_____

CINNAMON-COATED
CELEBRITIES

A
N
S
W
E
R
S

WAYANS
1. Marlon
2. Damon
3. Keenen
4. Shawn
5. Dwayne
6. Kim
7. Elvira
8. Deidra
9. Nadia
10. Vonnie

WINANS
1. Bebe
2. Cece
3. Angie
4. Debbie
5. Marvin
6. Carvin
7. Michael
8. Ronald
9. Vickie
10. Daniel

JACKSONS
1. Rebbie
2. Jackie
3. Tito
4. Jermaine
5. Marlon
6. Michael
7. Randy
8. Janet
9. LaToya

SENSATIONAL
SIBLINGS

CELEBRITIES

Put these famous Jackson brothers and sisters in order from oldest to youngest.

Jermaine	Michael	Randy
Tito	Rebbie	LaToya
Jackie	Marlon	Janet

1. _____

2. _____

3. _____

4. _____

5. _____

6. _____

7. _____

8. _____

9. _____

SENSATIONAL
SIBLINGS

1. Rebbie, born in 1950
2. Jackie, born in 1951
3. Tito, born in 1953
4. Jermaine, born in 1954
5. Marlon, born in 1957
6. LaToya, born in 1956
7. Michael, born in 1958
8. Randy, born in 1961
9. Janet, born in 1966

DADDY DEAREST

ESPECIALLY FOR THE BROTHERS

How well do you know the daddy-to-be? *Answer these ten questions.*

1. Birthday _____

2. Number of siblings _____

3. Shoe size _____

4. Number of children dad wants _____

5. Favorite sport _____

6. Favorite sports team _____

7. Year graduated from high school _____

8. Favorite color(s) _____

9. Birthplace _____

10. Job Title _____

DADDY DILEMMA

Using your knowledge of television shows, *match the names of the following characters with their proper children.*

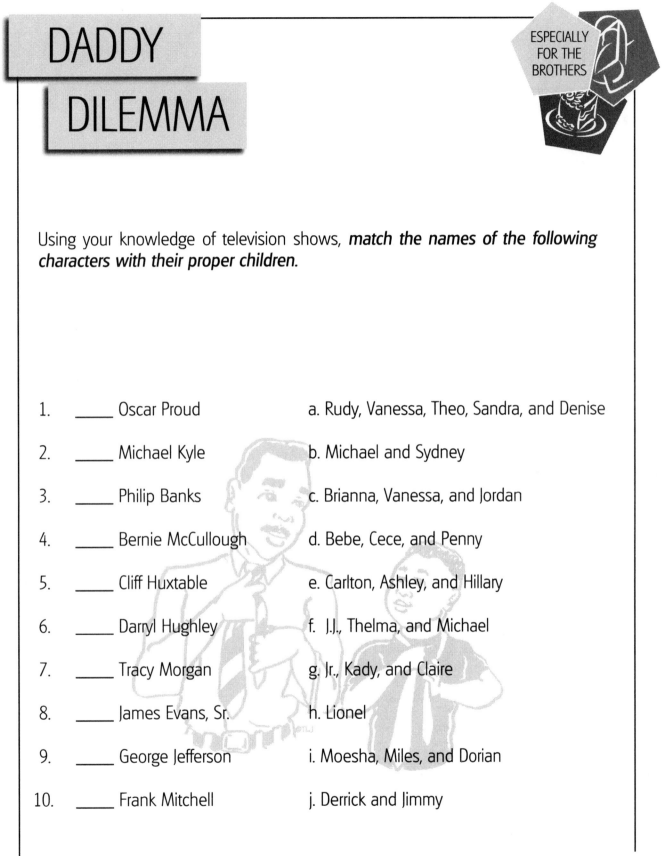

1. _____ Oscar Proud   a. Rudy, Vanessa, Theo, Sandra, and Denise

2. _____ Michael Kyle   b. Michael and Sydney

3. _____ Philip Banks   c. Brianna, Vanessa, and Jordan

4. _____ Bernie McCullough   d. Bebe, Cece, and Penny

5. _____ Cliff Huxtable   e. Carlton, Ashley, and Hillary

6. _____ Darryl Hughley   f. J.J., Thelma, and Michael

7. _____ Tracy Morgan   g. Jr., Kady, and Claire

8. _____ James Evans, Sr.   h. Lionel

9. _____ George Jefferson   i. Moesha, Miles, and Dorian

10. _____ Frank Mitchell   j. Derrick and Jimmy

DADDY
DILEMMA

ANSWERS

1. d. Bebe, Cece, and Penny
2. g. Jr., Kady, and Claire
3. e. Carlton, Ashley, and Hillary
4. c. Brianna, Vanessa, and Jordan
5. a. Rudy, Vanessa, Theo, Sandra, and Denise
6. b. Michael and Sydney
7. j. Derrick and Jimmy
8. f. J.J., Thelma, and Michael
9. h. Lionel
10. i. Moesha, Miles, and Dorian

TELEVISION CELEBRITY DADS

Using your knowledge of television shows, **match the titles of the following shows with the appropriate actor**s whose portrayal as "Dads" keeps us laughing.

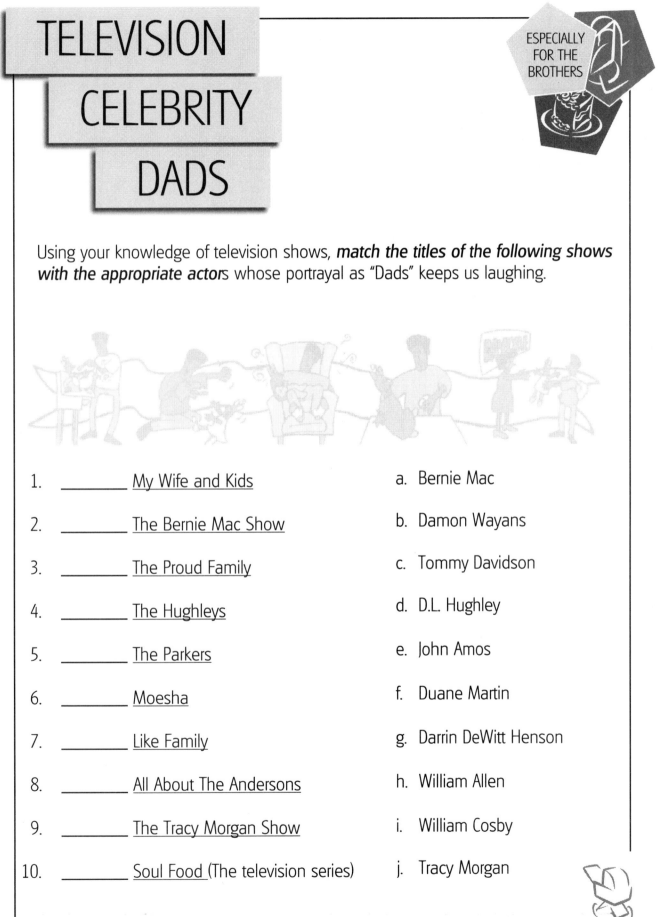

1. _____ <u>My Wife and Kids</u>

2. _____ <u>The Bernie Mac Show</u>

3. _____ <u>The Proud Family</u>

4. _____ <u>The Hughleys</u>

5. _____ <u>The Parkers</u>

6. _____ <u>Moesha</u>

7. _____ <u>Like Family</u>

8. _____ <u>All About The Andersons</u>

9. _____ <u>The Tracy Morgan Show</u>

10. _____ <u>Soul Food</u> (The television series)

a. Bernie Mac

b. Damon Wayans

c. Tommy Davidson

d. D.L. Hughley

e. John Amos

f. Duane Martin

g. Darrin DeWitt Henson

h. William Allen

i. William Cosby

j. Tracy Morgan

TELEVISION CELEBRITY DADS

ANSWERS

1.   b. Damon Wayans

2.   a. Bernie Mac

3.   c. Tommy Davidson

4.   d. D.L. Hughley

5.   i. William Cosby

6.   h. William Allen

7.   f. Duane Martin

8.   e. John Amos

9.   j. Tracy Morgan

10.   g. Darrin DeWitt Henson

ACROSS THE GLOBE

GLOBAL CULTURE

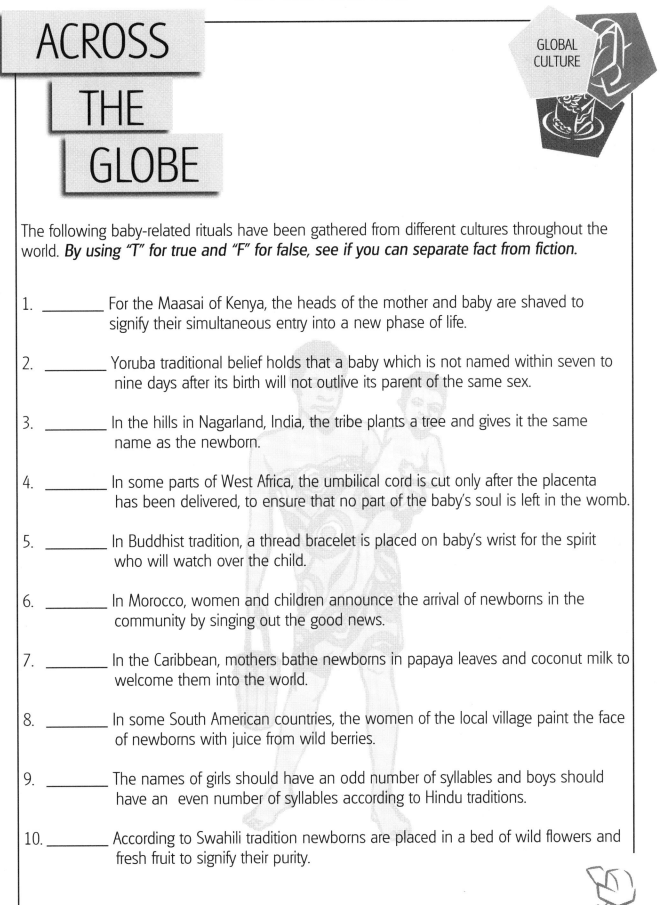

The following baby-related rituals have been gathered from different cultures throughout the world. **By using "T" for true and "F" for false, see if you can separate fact from fiction.**

1. _____ For the Maasai of Kenya, the heads of the mother and baby are shaved to signify their simultaneous entry into a new phase of life.

2. _____ Yoruba traditional belief holds that a baby which is not named within seven to nine days after its birth will not outlive its parent of the same sex.

3. _____ In the hills in Nagarland, India, the tribe plants a tree and gives it the same name as the newborn.

4. _____ In some parts of West Africa, the umbilical cord is cut only after the placenta has been delivered, to ensure that no part of the baby's soul is left in the womb.

5. _____ In Buddhist tradition, a thread bracelet is placed on baby's wrist for the spirit who will watch over the child.

6. _____ In Morocco, women and children announce the arrival of newborns in the community by singing out the good news.

7. _____ In the Caribbean, mothers bathe newborns in papaya leaves and coconut milk to welcome them into the world.

8. _____ In some South American countries, the women of the local village paint the face of newborns with juice from wild berries.

9. _____ The names of girls should have an odd number of syllables and boys should have an even number of syllables according to Hindu traditions.

10. _____ According to Swahili tradition newborns are placed in a bed of wild flowers and fresh fruit to signify their purity.

ACROSS THE GLOBE

ANSWERS

1. TRUE
2. TRUE
3. TRUE
4. TRUE
5. TRUE
6. TRUE
7. FALSE
8. FALSE
9. TRUE
10. FALSE

SOURCES
1. http://www.vishnumandir.com/htm/sams5.htm
   http://www.washingtonparent.com/articles/0107/welcoming.htm
2. http://www.folklife.si.edu/vfest/africa/photo2.htm
3. African Ceremonies. Photo: Carol Beckwith & Angela Fisher, courtesy of Abrams

LABOR
AND DELIVERY
RITUALS

GLOBAL CULTURE

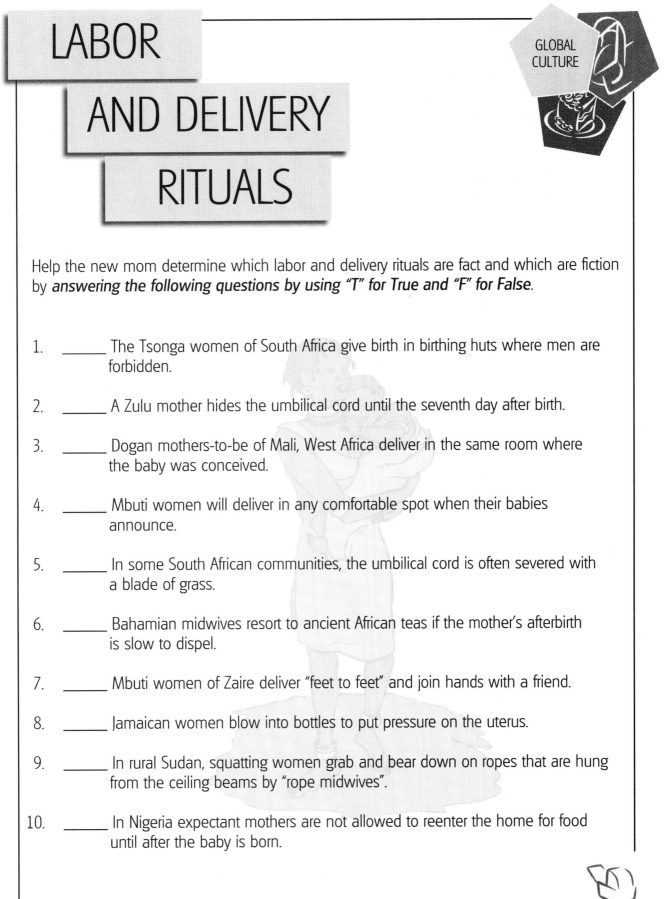

Help the new mom determine which labor and delivery rituals are fact and which are fiction by *answering the following questions by using "T" for True and "F" for False*.

1. _____ The Tsonga women of South Africa give birth in birthing huts where men are forbidden.

2. _____ A Zulu mother hides the umbilical cord until the seventh day after birth.

3. _____ Dogan mothers-to-be of Mali, West Africa deliver in the same room where the baby was conceived.

4. _____ Mbuti women will deliver in any comfortable spot when their babies announce.

5. _____ In some South African communities, the umbilical cord is often severed with a blade of grass.

6. _____ Bahamian midwives resort to ancient African teas if the mother's afterbirth is slow to dispel.

7. _____ Mbuti women of Zaire deliver "feet to feet" and join hands with a friend.

8. _____ Jamaican women blow into bottles to put pressure on the uterus.

9. _____ In rural Sudan, squatting women grab and bear down on ropes that are hung from the ceiling beams by "rope midwives".

10. _____ In Nigeria expectant mothers are not allowed to reenter the home for food until after the baby is born.

LABOR
AND DELIVERY
RITUALS

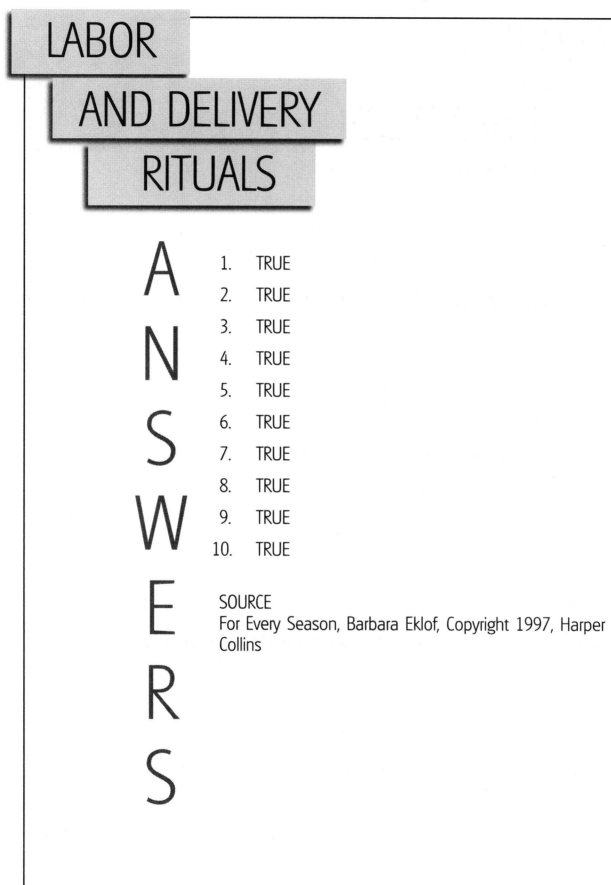

A
N
S
W
E
R
S

1. TRUE
2. TRUE
3. TRUE
4. TRUE
5. TRUE
6. TRUE
7. TRUE
8. TRUE
9. TRUE
10. TRUE

SOURCE
For Every Season, Barbara Eklof, Copyright 1997, Harper Collins

COLORFUL
CHARACTERS

NURSERY RHYMES

How well do you remember these "colorful" characters?

Fill in the blanks with the colors found in popular nursery rhymes and children's stories.

1. Baa, Baa, _____ sheep, have you any wool?

2. Snow _____ lived with the seven dwarves.

3. Little _____ Riding Hood went through the woods to Grandma's house.

4. Roses are _____. Violets are _____. Sugar is sweet and so are you.

5. Hickety, pickety, my _____ hen. She lays eggs for gentlemen.

6. Little boy _____ come blow your horn. The sheep are in the meadow ...

7. Dr. Seuss' Sam-I-Am ate _____ eggs and ham.

8. Mary had a little lamb; its fleece was _____ as snow.

9. Mary, Mary, quite contrary, How does your garden grow? With _____ bells and cockleshells...

10. Sing a song of sixpence, a pocket full of rye, four and twenty _____ birds baked in a pie.

COLORFUL CHARACTERS

ANSWERS

1. black
2. white
3. red
4. red, blue
5. black
6. blue
7. green
8. white
9. silver
10. black

NURSERY

NUMBERS

NURSERY
RHYMES

Using your knowledge of nursery rhymes and children's stories, *answer the following questions.*

1. _____ Number of Dalmatians in the Disney classic tale "___ Dalmatians".

2. _____ Number of pigs whose houses were blown down by the Big, Bad Wolf.

3. _____ Number of bears in the story with Goldilocks.

4. _____ Number of dwarves living with Snow White.

5. _____ Number of kittens that lost their mittens.

6. _____ Number of blind mice.

7. _____ Number of bags of wool owned by Baa, baa black sheep.

8. _____ Number of lambs that followed Mary to school one day.

9. _____ Number of days pease porridge was in the pot.

10. _____ Number of white horses she'll be drivin', when she'll be comin' round the mountain.

NURSERY NUMBERS

ANSWERS

1. 101
2. 2
3. 3
4. 7
5. 3
6. 3
7. 3
8. 1
9. 9
10. 6

WHO SAID THAT?

The following characters from popular nursery rhymes and short stories are listed below.

Match the character with the appropriate quote or phrase.

Jack Sprat	Baby Bear	Jack and Jill
Big Bad Wolf	Gingerbread Man	Little Bo Peep
Georgie Porgie	The Little Teapot	Humpty Dumpty
	Old Mother Hubbard	

1. _____ "I'll huff and puff and blow your house down".

2. _____ He could eat no fat, his wife could eat no lean.

3. _____ "Run, run as fast as you can. You can't catch me ..."

4. _____ "Someone's been eating my porridge, and it's all gone."

5. _____ Who kissed the girls and made them cry?

6. _____ Who sat on a wall and had a great fall?

7. _____ "Here is my handle, here is spout."

8. _____ Who went up the hill to fetch a pail of water?

9. _____ Who lost her sheep and didn't know where to find them?

10. _____ She went to the cupboard to get her poor dog a bone.

WHO SAID THAT?

ANSWERS

1. Big Bad Wolf

2. Jack Sprat

3. Gingerbread man

4. Baby Bear

5. Georgie Porgie

6. Humpty Dumpty

7. The Little Teapot

8. Jack and Jill

9. Little Bo Peep

10. Old Mother Hubbard

TELEVISION CELEBRITY MOMS

Using your knowledge of television shows, **match the titles of the following shows with the correct actresses** whose portrayal as "Moms" keeps us laughing.

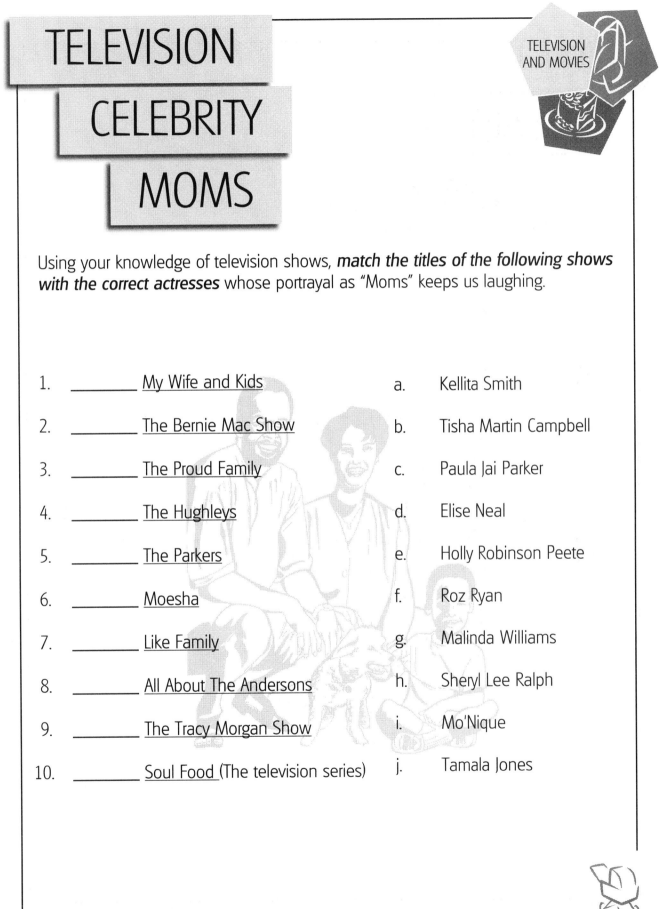

1. _____ <u>My Wife and Kids</u>   a.   Kellita Smith

2. _____ <u>The Bernie Mac Show</u>   b.   Tisha Martin Campbell

3. _____ <u>The Proud Family</u>   c.   Paula Jai Parker

4. _____ <u>The Hughleys</u>   d.   Elise Neal

5. _____ <u>The Parkers</u>   e.   Holly Robinson Peete

6. _____ <u>Moesha</u>   f.   Roz Ryan

7. _____ <u>Like Family</u>   g.   Malinda Williams

8. _____ <u>All About The Andersons</u>   h.   Sheryl Lee Ralph

9. _____ <u>The Tracy Morgan Show</u>   i.   Mo'Nique

10. _____ <u>Soul Food</u> (The television series)   j.   Tamala Jones

TELEVISION CELEBRITY MOMS

ANSWERS

1. b.   Tisha Martin Campbell
2. a.   Kellita Smith
3. c.   Paula Jai Parker
4. d.   Elise Neal
5. i.   Mo'Nique
6. h.   Sheryl Lee Ralph
7. e.   Holly Robinson Peete
8. f.   Roz Ryan
9. j.   Tamala Jones
10. g. Malinda Williams

TELEVISION

NUMBERS

TELEVISION
AND MOVIES

Using your knowledge of television shows, *answer the following questions.*

1. _____ Number of children that James and Florida had on <u>Good Times</u>.

2. _____ Number of children that Michael and Jay Kyle had on <u>My Wife and Kids</u>.

3. _____ Number of children that Heathcliff and Claire Huxtable had on <u>The Cosby Show</u>.

4. _____ Number of children that George and Louise Jefferson had on <u>The Jeffersons</u>.

5. _____ Number of children raised by Frank and Dee Mitchell on <u>Moesha</u>.

6. _____ Number of children raised by Bernie and Wanda McCullough on <u>The Bernie Mac Show</u>.

7. _____ Number of children living with Phil and Vivian Banks on <u>The Fresh Prince of Bel Air</u>.

8. _____ Number of children that Oscar and Trudy Proud have on <u>The Proud Family</u>.

9. _____ Number of children living with Robert and Jerri Peterson on <u>The Parent 'Hood</u>.

10. _____ Number of children that Darryl and Yvonne Hughley have on <u>The Hughleys</u>.

TELEVISION
NUMBERS

A
N
S
W
E
R
S

1. 3 - Michael, Thelma, and J.J.
2. 3 - Jr., Kady, and Claire
3. 5 - Rudy, Vanessa, Theo, Sandra, and Denise
4. 1 - Lionel
5. 3 - Moesha, Miles, and Dorian
6. 3 - Brianna, Vanessa, and Jordan
7. 4 - Carlton, Ashley, Hillary, and Will
8. 3 - Bebe, Cece, and Penny
9. 5 - Cece, Zaira, Nicholas, Michael, and T.K.
10. 2 - Michael and Sydney

TINY TOTS TELEVISION

TELEVISION AND MOVIES

Help mom to learn the television characters that her youngster will find fascinating.

Match the television show to its proper characters.

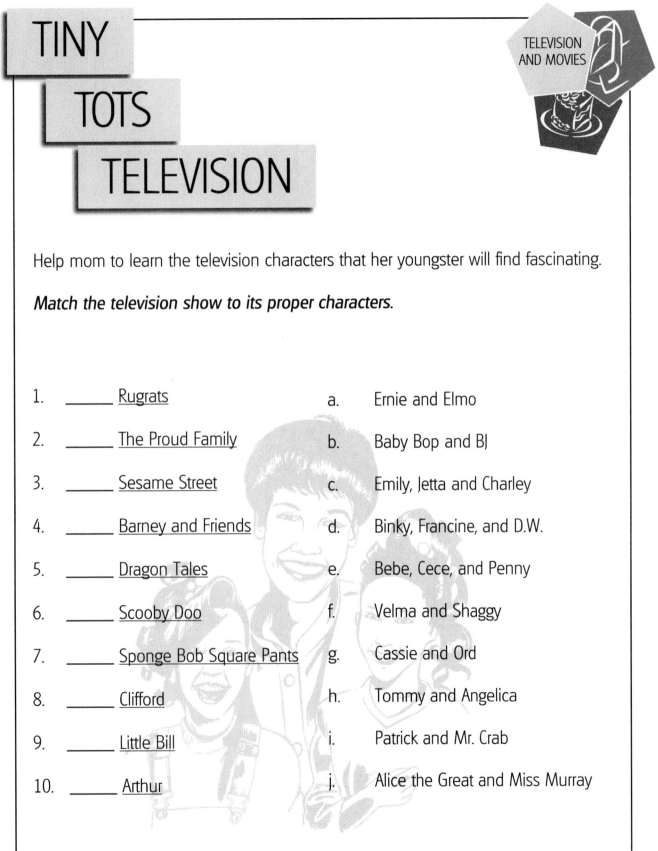

1. _____ Rugrats

2. _____ The Proud Family

3. _____ Sesame Street

4. _____ Barney and Friends

5. _____ Dragon Tales

6. _____ Scooby Doo

7. _____ Sponge Bob Square Pants

8. _____ Clifford

9. _____ Little Bill

10. _____ Arthur

a. Ernie and Elmo

b. Baby Bop and BJ

c. Emily, Jetta and Charley

d. Binky, Francine, and D.W.

e. Bebe, Cece, and Penny

f. Velma and Shaggy

g. Cassie and Ord

h. Tommy and Angelica

i. Patrick and Mr. Crab

j. Alice the Great and Miss Murray

TINY
TOTS
TELEVISION

A
N
S
W
E
R
S

1.   h.   Tommy and Angelica ®™ Nickelodeon
2.   e.   Bebe, Cece, and Penny ®™ Disney
3.   a.   Ernie and Elmo ®™ PBS
4.   b.   Baby Bop and BJ ®™ PBS
5.   g.   Cassie and Ord   ®™ PBS
6.   f.   Velma and Shaggy
7.   i.   Patrick and Mr. Crab ®™ Nickelodeon
8.   c.   Emily, Jetta and Charley ®™ PBS
9.   j.   Alice the Great and Miss Murray ®™   Nickelodeon,
10.   d.   Binky, Francine, and D.W. ®™ PBS

AROUND THE TUMMY

TRADITIONAL

See who can guess the correct size of mommy's tummy.

For this game you will need either a ball of string, toilet paper or yarn and a pair of scissors.

Pass the ball of string and the scissors to each guest. He or she should cut off a piece of string guessing a length to fit around the Mother's tummy. Mom will then try on each piece of string.

The guest with the closest length to mommy's tummy will be the winner.

BABY FACT

OR FICTION?

What's the real deal?

Lots of us have heard things about babies and wondered if they were true or not.

Help the new mom *separate fact from fiction by answering the following questions.*

1. _____ Babies should be put to sleep on their tummies.

2. _____ Too much caffeine may contribute to the risk of having a low-birth weight baby.

3. _____ Car seats can be placed safely in the front or back seat of the vehicle.

4. _____ Remove pillows, quilts, comforters, sheepskins, stuffed toys, and other soft products from the crib when baby is sleeping.

5. _____ Many pediatricians suggest waiting until your baby is at least 6 months old before feeding solid foods.

6. _____ Baby is born with very poor vision but can recognize his/her mother almost right away.

7. _____ A baby or toddler can drown in less than an inch of water.

8. _____ A woman created the first diaper.

9. _____ A woman started Mother's Day.

10. _____ When cooking, all pot handles should be in towards the stove so baby can not reach them.

BABY FACT
OR FICTION?

A
N
S
W
E
R
S

1.   FALSE

2.   TRUE

3.   FALSE

4.   TRUE

5.   TRUE

6.   TRUE

7.   TRUE

8.   FALSE

9.   TRUE

10. TRUE

BABY
HODGEPODGE

TRADITIONAL

New moms will find the following baby related items helpful.

Unscramble each word to find out what they are.

1. LEROLSRT _____

2. RICB _____

3. PENYAYLP _____

4. PAERID _____

5. NKELABT _____

6. IBB _____

7. GHIH AIRHC _____

8. OLTBTE _____

9. ARC ATES _____

10. AYBB OWPDER _____

BABY

HODGEPODGE

A
N
S
W
E
R
S

1. STROLLER
2. CRIB
3. PLAYPEN
4. DIAPER
5. BLANKET
6. BIB
7. HIGH CHAIR
8. BOTTLE
9. CAR SEAT
10. BABY POWDER

BABY SONG
MUSICAL
CHAIRS

TRADITIONAL

See who is left standing after playing musical chairs to baby music!

For this game you'll need to select a compact disc (CD) or tape of baby music and have a CD or tape player handy. Don't let your guests see when you are going to turn the music off.

Set up fewer chairs in the middle of the room than you have players, and have them walk around the chairs while you play the music. Abruptly stop the music and watch your guests scramble for a seat. Those left standing are out of the game. Remove one chair after each round and the last person standing wins the game.

This game is especially fun to play when children are included at the shower.

CHARADES

TRADITIONAL

See who is an actor in the making!

For this game you will need a timer with a buzzer, a few sheets of paper and a hat or other object to hold the sheets of paper.

Write down baby themed actions (such as changing a diaper, burping baby, rocking baby) on small slips of paper. Fold each slip in half and put in a hat. Have guests take turns drawing the sheets out of the hat, then act out the action described on the paper. Guests are not allowed to speak but are free to use their hands or other objects. Set the timer as the guests begin their acting debut. If no one guesses the action before the buzzer goes off the actor will have to select another action to perform for the crowd.

This game can be played in teams if you have a large shower or if you are having a couple's shower. Simply award points to the people that have guessed correctly within the time allowed. The person with the most points wins.

GRANDMA'S
ADVICE

TRADITIONAL

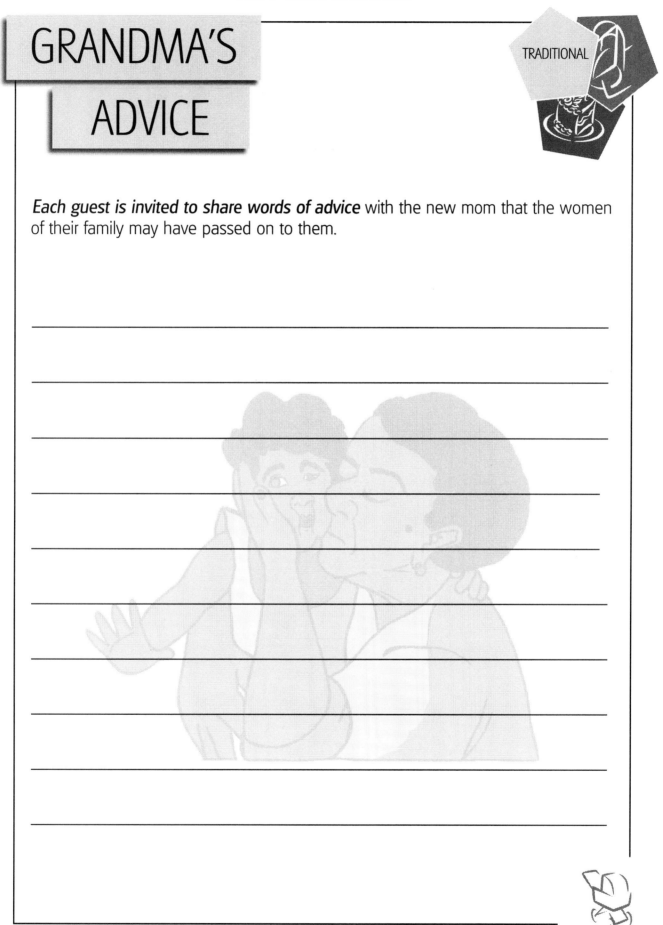

Each guest is invited to share words of advice with the new mom that the women of their family may have passed on to them.

MEMORY
CHALLENGE

TRADITIONAL

See how many items you can memorize.

Study the pictures for 30 seconds then turn over the paper and list as many of the objects you can remember.

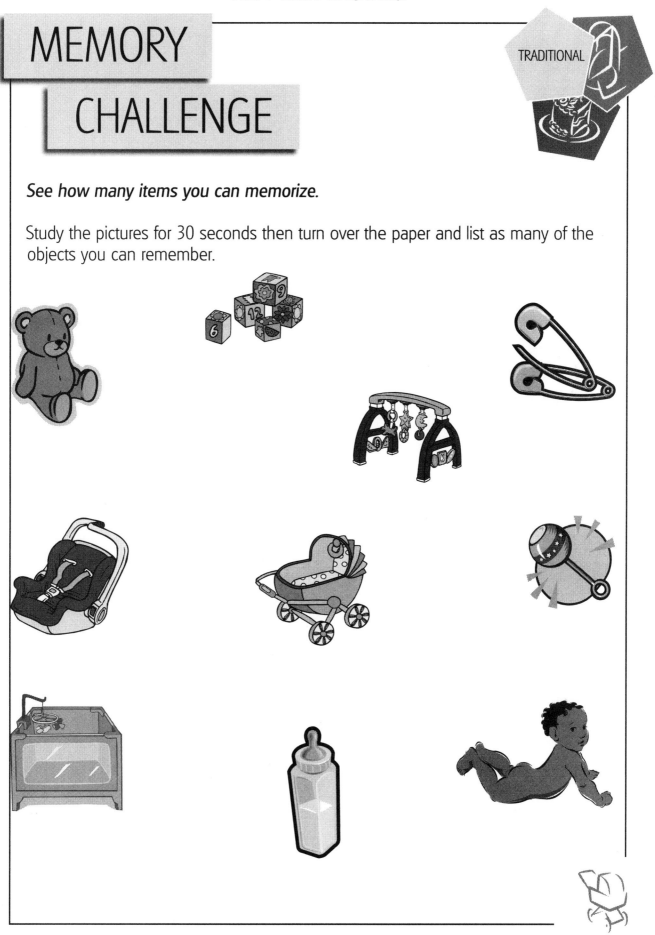

MEMORY
CHALLENGE

_____

_____

_____

_____

_____

_____

_____

ANSWER
safety pins, stroller, mobile, playpen, baby bottle, rattle, baby blocks, car seat, bear, baby

MOMMY
MYSTERY

TRADITIONAL

How well do you know the mother-to-be?

Answer these ten questions.

1. Birthday _____

2. Number of brothers and sisters _____

3. Shoe size _____

4. Number of children mom wants _____

5. Number of pounds gained during pregnancy _____

6. Craved food(s) _____

7. Hospital the baby will be born in _____

8. Favorite colors _____

9. Birthplace _____

10. Sex of the baby _____

NAME THE BABY

Using only the first initial in the names of the parents, *see how many names for the baby can be created.*

For example, if Mom's first name is Karen then list baby names starting with the letter "K".

_____   _____
Mother's first initial   *Father's first initial*

_____   _____

_____   _____

_____   _____

_____   _____

_____   _____

_____   _____

_____   _____

NIGHTTIME NIBBLING

TRADITIONAL

Solve the puzzle to find out why this man is making a peanut butter and sardine sandwich at such an early hour of the morning.

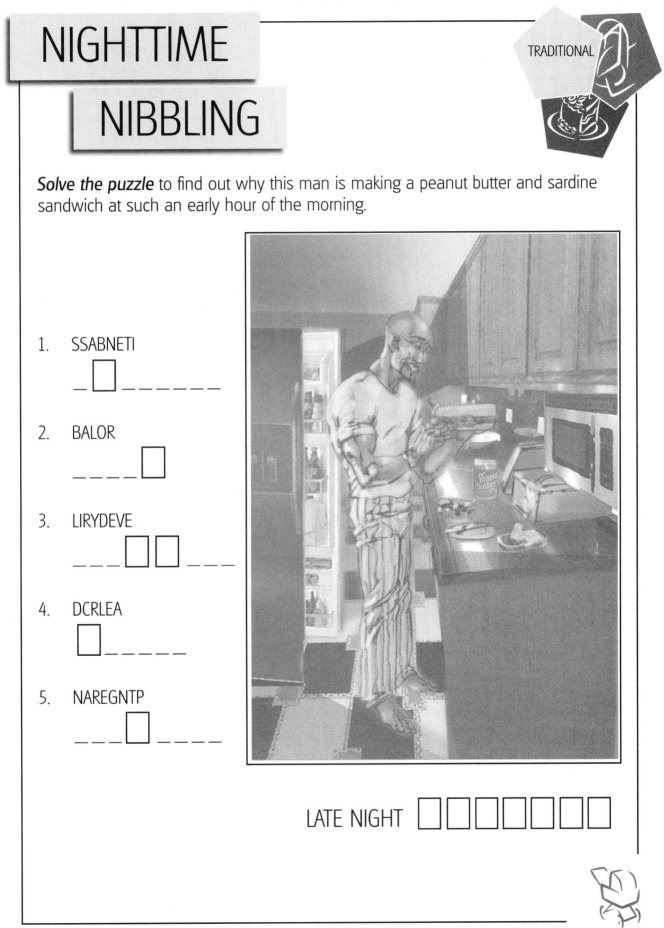

1. SSABNETI

   _ [ ] _ _ _ _ _ _

2. BALOR

   _ _ _ _ [ ]

3. LIRYDEVE

   _ _ _ [ ] [ ] _ _ _

4. DCRLEA

   [ ] _ _ _ _ _

5. NAREGNTP

   _ _ _ [ ] _ _ _ _

LATE NIGHT [ ] [ ] [ ] [ ] [ ] [ ] [ ]

NIGHTTIME NIBBLING

A
N
S
W
E
R
S

1. BASSINET
2. LABOR
3. DELIVERY
4. CRADLE
5. PREGNANT

LATE NIGHT CRAVING

PASS THE BABY

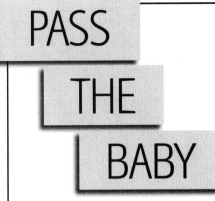

TRADITIONAL

See who is left holding the baby after the timer goes off!

This game is played the same way as the traditional hot potato game with a few small exceptions. You'll need a child's toy baby or doll and a timer with a buzzer.

You can either have your guests stand or place their chairs in a small circle. Use the child's toy baby or doll as the potato. Set the timer for less than a minute and have guests pass the baby around the circle until the buzzer sounds. The guest left holding the baby when the timer sounds is out of the game. That person should either step out or remove their chair from the circle. If someone drops the baby they are also out. Once two players remain and the final buzzer sounds the person not holding the baby wins the game.

This game will be a hit with the children at the shower.

SAY
CHEESE!

See which guest can identify the most baby pictures.

For this shower you will need your guests to bring a picture of himself or herself as a baby or child and a large poster.

As each guest arrives take his or her picture and add it to the poster using tape, making sure to number each picture. Don't let anyone else see the poster until it's time to play the game.

Later on in the party, bring out the poster and using the game sheet included have your guests write down the name of the person whom they think is in the photograph next to the corresponding number. The person with the most correct guesses win.

SAY
CHEESE!

Photo 1	_____	Photo 16	_____
Photo 2	_____	Photo 17	_____
Photo 3	_____	Photo 18	_____
Photo 4	_____	Photo 19	_____
Photo 5	_____	Photo 20	_____
Photo 6	_____	Photo 21	_____
Photo 7	_____	Photo 22	_____
Photo 8	_____	Photo 23	_____
Photo 9	_____	Photo 24	_____
Photo 10	_____	Photo 25	_____
Photo 11	_____	Photo 26	_____
Photo 12	_____	Photo 27	_____
Photo 13	_____	Photo 28	_____
Photo 14	_____	Photo 29	_____
Photo 15	_____	Photo 30	_____

SHOE FETISH

TRADITIONAL

As this expectant mom searches through the closet to find a pair of matching shoes, **solve the puzzle** to determine what she has also not seen in at least two months.

1. CIPAERFI

_ _ _ ☐ _ _ ☐

2. ERLKAW

_ _ _ _ ☐ _

3. TLEBOT

_ _ ☐ _ _ ☐

4. RHSA

_ _ _ ☐

5. VELIRED

_ ☐ _ _ _ _ _

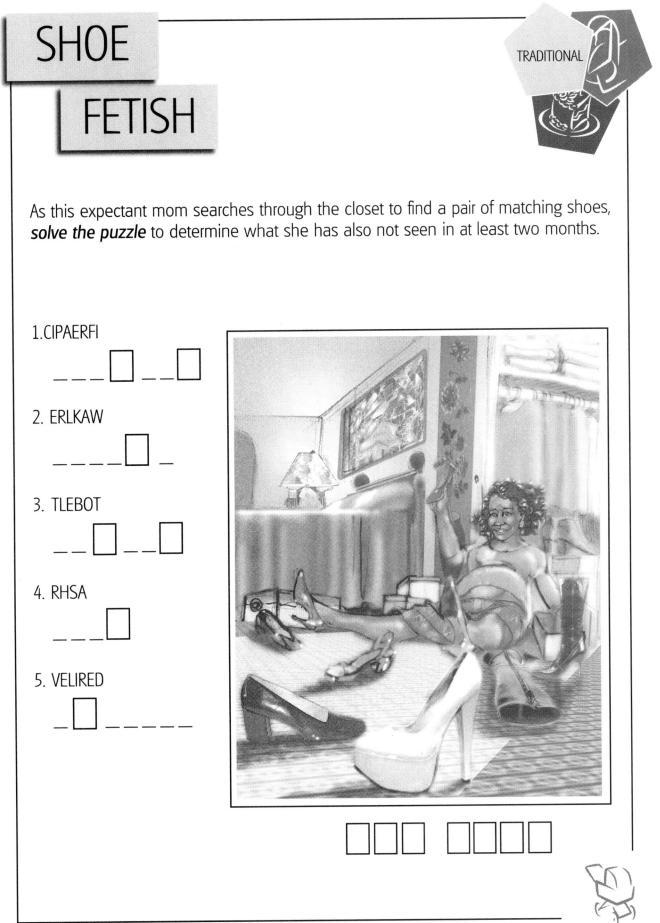

☐☐☐ ☐☐☐☐

163

SHOE
FETISH

ANSWERS

1. PACIFIER
2. WALKER
3. BOTTLE
4. RASH
5. TEETHING

HER FEET

WHAT'S IN MOMMY'S BABY BAG?

TRADITIONAL

Moms always seem to carry around a lot of things that their new baby will need.

List the things you think may be in mom's baby bag.

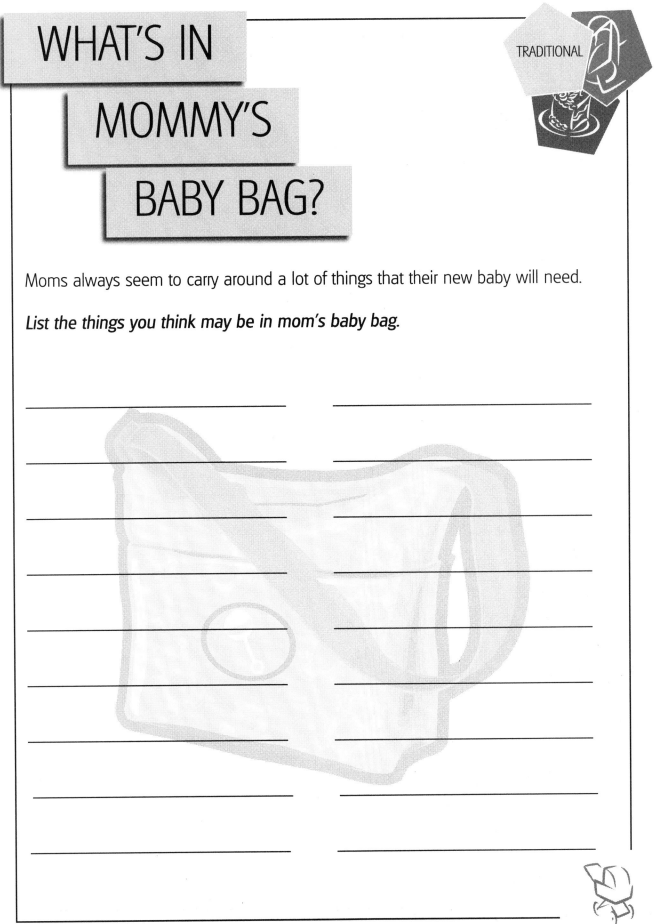

_____   _____

_____   _____

_____   _____

_____   _____

_____   _____

_____   _____

_____   _____

Part 4
RESOURCES

The final ingredients needed for a successful shower
are included in this section. The worksheets provided
will ensure the previous ingredients blend easily.

Shopping List

Notes:

Budget Planning Worksheet

Notes:

ITEM	BUDGETED AMOUNT ($)	ACTUAL AMOUNT ($)
	TOTAL =	TOTAL =

Location Planning Worksheet

Name of place: _____

Address: _____

Distance from guest-of-honor's home: _____

Total number of people expected: _____ Adults _____ Children _____

Type of food: _____

Average cost per meal: _____

Attire/dress code: _____

Decorations allowed   YES ☐   NO ☐

Private party room available   YES ☐   NO ☐

Reserve seating available   YES ☐   NO ☐

Accessible by public transportation   YES ☐   NO ☐

Other: _____
_____
_____

PROS:

CONS:

LOCATION SELECTED:

YES ☐   NO ☐

Guest List Worksheet

Name: _____

Address: _____

Phone number: _____

E-mail address: _____

Relationship to guest-of-honor: _____

Total number of people invited: _____ Adults _____ Children _____

If children will attend what age(s): _____

Invitation sent on _____

R.S.V.P. by _____ R.S.V.P. received   YES ☐   NO ☐
       (Date)

Gift given: _____

Thank you card sent on: _____

Name: _____

Address: _____

Phone number: _____

E-mail address: _____

Relationship to guest-of-honor: _____

Total number of people invited: _____ Adults _____ Children _____

If children will attend what age(s): _____

Invitation sent on _____

R.S.V.P. by _____ R.S.V.P. received   YES ☐   NO ☐
       (Date)

Gift given: _____

Thank you card sent on: _____

Bridal and Baby Shower Resources

BRIDAL AND BABY SHOWER ACCESSORIES
Carole Joy Creations, Inc.®
A 100% Black Owned Company
6 Production Drive, Unit 1, Brookfield CT 06804
http://www.carolejoy.com
TEL (203) 740-4490 • FAX (203) 740-4495
Phone Orders (800) 223-6945
Baby's heritage book, gift-wrap, birth announcements, and shower invitations.

BABY SHOWER ACCESSORIES
Sugar's Babies, LLC
15507 So. Normandie Ave. #434
Gardena, CA 90247
Toll-Free (877) 679-3389
http://www.sugarsbabies.com
Sugar's Babies is an African-American family-owned business established to manufacture nursery decor and room accessories, especially crib bedding, celebrating children of color.

WOMENS' RESOURCES
Nia Online
23 West Hubbard St.
Suite 200
Chicago, Illinois 60610
http://niaonline.com
TEL (312) 222-0943 • FAX (312) 222-0944
NiaOnline offers harmonious, purposeful living through its use of community-building content and convenient, personalized online shopping.

Mocha Moms
http://www.mochamoms.org/
Mocha Moms is a support group for stay at home mothers of color who have chosen not to work full-time outside of the home in order to devote more time to their families.

Mommy Too! Magazine
http://www.mommytoo.com
Established in October 2003, Mommy Too! Magazine is a fresh, new web magazine designed to be the premier online portal and publication for motherhood and mothering for mothers of color in the country.

BRIDAL SHOWERS ACCESSORIES
African American Roots, Inc.
8702 Driftwood Drive Suite A
Tampa, FL 33615
TEL (813) 884-8923 • FAX (813) 884-8941
Toll-Free 888-523-0091
http://african-weddings.com/
Largest and most unique selections of ceremonial wedding brooms and accompanying favors available.

BRIDAL SHOWS
Black & Beautiful Wedding Expo
PO Box 5951
Hampton Park, MD 20791-5951
http://www.blackbeautifulwedding.com
TEL 301-780-9003/Event Line
TOLL-FREE 1-800-930-BBWE (2293)
African-American bridal shows in the Washington, DC metropolitan area.

The African-American Wedding Expo (AAWE)
http://www.africanamericanweddingexpo.com
TEL 904-764-7828 • FAX 1-866-764-7944
TOLL-FREE 1-877-249-6399
African-American bridal show in Jacksonville, Florida.

World of Weddings (WOW)
1635 Old Hwy 41
Suite 1112-340
Kennesaw. GA 30152
http://www.worldofweddings.net
TEL (770) 420-8983
Show located in Atlanta, Georgia.
The WOW Expo is the first wedding show of its kind to celebrate the different cultures (American, African American, Hispanic, Asian, India, Caribbean, and much more) under one roof.

Twice Is Nice Bridal Creations LLC
5600 Sunpath Circle
Charlotte, NC 28269
TEL (704) 509-0702
http://www.twiceisnicebride.com
Show located in Charlotte, NC.
Twice is Nice provides services that help deal with challenges that comes from a subsequent marriage.

Bridal and Baby Shower Resources

ONLINE WEDDING RESOURCES
VIBRIDE.COM
http://www.vibride.com/
Vibride.com offers free advice, information, money saving tips and great ways to personalize your wedding. Offers African favors, wedding gowns, and an on-line black bridal community.

Black Bride
www.blackbride.com
Black Bride offers African American wedding information from companies that meet a black couples needs and wants the couples business.

African Wedding Guide
http://www.africanweddingguide.com
The African Wedding Guide is an inclusive online resource to assist you in planning either an African-inspired or traditional wedding.

Ebony Bridal Planner
http://www.ebonybridalplanner.com
African American wedding invitations, African American wedding dress, African American wedding music, and much more!

Maryland Black Weddings
http://www.mdblackweddings.com
Maryland Black Weddings provides listings of weddings professionals from Maryland, Virginia and Washington DC.

African-American Brides – Yahoo! Group
http://groups.yahoo.com/group/africanamericanbrides/
Yahoo club where African-American brides-to-be, newlyweds, and marriage veterans discuss weddings and marriage in general.

BRIDAL GOWNS
Cassandra Bromfield
http://www.cassandrabromfield.com
Cassandra Bromfield's creative, traditional and African American Inspired Designs Have graced the pages of some of the top bridal and fashion magazine.

ONLINE WEDDING AND BABY RESOURCES
Cushcity.com
http://www.cushcity.com
Offers a selection of both wedding and baby items: books, cake toppers, invitations.

Gift Certificates

Gift Certificate

BlackBerry Soul

Presented to _____

On _____

For _____

Congratulations,

From _____

Gift Certificate

BlackBerry Soul

Presented to _____

On _____

For _____

Congratulations,

From _____

Author Information

Kimberly K. Smith was born on St. Croix, U.S. Virgin Islands where she enjoyed the crystal blue waters and white sandy beaches of the tropics. The younger of two siblings, Kimberly left the islands after completing high school to attend North Carolina A&T State University where she graduated with a Bachelor's Degree in Engineering.   While living in Alexandria, Virginia she continued her educational pursuit by completing her Master's Degree in Management. She has worked for the federal government in Washington, DC for more than ten years.

Kimberly was motivated to write **BlackBerry Soul Celebrations** after attending several bridal and baby showers including her own. Noticing the lack of games that reflected the lives and experiences of her friends and family, she was inspired to create a book that focused on the things that touched her life.

She currently resides in a suburb outside of Washington, DC with her husband, Reggie, son, Kyle and is awaiting the birth of a baby boy in February 2005.

For more information visit **www.blackberrysoul.com**